MW01697767

Missouri's Wild
MUSHROOMS

by

Maxine Stone

Copyright © 2010, 2012 by the Conservation Commission of the State of Missouri

ISBN 978-1-887247-74-0

Published by the Missouri Department of Conservation
P.O. Box 180, Jefferson City, Missouri 65102-1080

Equal opportunity to participate in and benefit from programs of the Missouri Department of Conservation is available to all individuals without regard to their race, color, national origin, sex, age or disability. Questions should be directed to the Department of Conservation, P.O. Box 180, Jefferson City, MO 65102, (573) 751-4115 (voice) or 800-735-2966 (TTY), or to the U.S. Fish and Wildlife Service Division of Federal Assistance, 4401 N. Fairfax Drive, Mail Stop: MBSP-4020, Arlington, VA 22203.

Missouri's Wild
MUSHROOMS

by

Maxine Stone

MISSOURI CONSERVATION DEPARTMENT

Serving nature and you®

Chlorophyllum molybdites, p. 46

Caution!

If you choose to eat wild mushrooms, safety should be your first concern. Never forget that some mushrooms are deadly, and never eat a mushroom that has not been positively identified. If you cannot positively identify a mushroom that you want to eat, take it to an expert. Neither the author nor the Missouri Department of Conservation can be responsible for the use or misuse of information in this book.

Barbara Bassett, Editor
Marci Porter, Designer

Photographs by Steve Adams, Brad Bomanz, Johann Bruhn, Jim Cooper, Bernadette Dryden, Tim Gleason, Patrick Harvey, Stan Hudson, Jay Justice, Michael Kuo, Patrick Lennon, Gordon Maupin, Joe McFarland, Noppadol Paothong, Joseph Rainwater, Jon Rapp, Maxine Stone, David Stonner, Cliff White, Catherine Williamson, David Yates

Front cover: *Pleurotus ostreatus* by Jon Rapp
Back cover: *Lactarius indigo* and *Cantharellus cinnabarinus* by Catherine Williamson

Table of Contents

Introduction

Flammulina velutipes, p. 30

If I can do it, you can do it!

It's true. I never thought I'd be a passionate mushroom hunter and mushroom lover. I never thought people would be calling me for expert mushroom advice. Never did I imagine that I'd be writing a field guide to Missouri mushrooms.

My story goes something like this…

I've spent a lot of time in the woods and have a deep admiration for nature's wonders. I've studied the names of plants, wildflowers and trees and enjoyed learning about them. When walking in the woods, I'd see ordinary mushrooms, beautiful mushrooms, and fantastic mushrooms, but I knew almost nothing about them. After checking field guides and studying on my own, I realized that identifying and understanding these weird-looking things was no easy task. Then I found the Missouri Mycological Society (MOMS). It was love at first foray. Oh, I had fun. And, oh, did I ever learn mushrooms.

The first year I joined MOMS, I took a series of monthly classes on mushroom identification and mushroom hunting. This helped me along quite a bit, but there are a lot of mushrooms out there and my learning was slow. I just kept at it. My first group foray was in the fall, and it was an absolute joy. There were mushrooms everywhere. At my first Winter Luncheon I realized that mushroom people were not only terrific folks, but like me, they also had a love of excellent food. Learning about mushrooms, hunting for mushrooms, eating mushrooms and being with other mushroom people was an incredibly fulfilling experience for me.

Learning Latin names and even some common names didn't come easy. I told myself that studying mycology was going to be fun, so I didn't sit down with lists and memorize names. Instead, I let my brain absorb what it wanted. To my surprise, it did. I am not a professional **mycologist**, but I am definitely a **mycophile**, someone who loves hunting and learning about mushrooms. Though some may call me an expert, there is too much that I don't know for me to give myself that title. But I do love everything about mushrooms, from hunting to identifying to eating. And here I am writing a field guide to mushrooms!

Each of you can discover your niche in life. Perhaps, like me, you will find wild mushrooms growing in it!

Acknowledgments

What a process this has been! Writing a book can be quite lonely. There are many hours at the computer, and then many more hours, and then many more! However, during the nearly three years it has taken to write this book, I have had numerous people come to my assistance with their expertise and their caring.

I would like to thank my dear friends Jay Justice and Brad Bomanz, who proofread the technical material in this book and assisted me throughout its writing.

I owe a great deal of thanks to my dear friends Carol Porter and Jane House, who proofread the non-technical parts of the book and always had an available ear and an encouraging word.

Deepest thanks to my talented photographers. They include Cliff, Dave and Nop with the Department of Conservation, and my many friends who took pictures and generously sent them to me for inclusion in this field guide. They are the best!

My book editor, Barbara Bassett, has been amazingly organized and patient, always helping me to stay consistent! My sincere thanks to Barbara.

Bernadette Dryden, publications editor with the Department of Conservation, was the driving force behind this project. This field guide never would have happened without her gracious, trusting and generous support. I also owe abundant thanks to Marci Porter, graphic designer at MDC, who made my words come to life.

All of my family have been loving and understanding when I've needed them. My daughters Deanna, Meredith and Sara, and my grandchildren Tiera, Michael and Morgan, have patiently given me encouragement, time and space. My sister Susan gave me hope when I thought I couldn't think any more. My numerous and wonderful friends have been great listeners and perfect cheerleaders. Heartfelt thanks also goes to Claudia Joyce, who introduced me to the Missouri Mycological Society (MOMS) many, many years ago.

I would never have written this field guide without the Missouri Mycological Society. MOMS changed my life. For everything from fascinating lessons about fungi to lifelong friendships, I give my loving gratitude to MOMS.

Catherine Williamson

Cliff White

Morchella esculenta, p. 109

SECTION I

Hunting

Missourians hunt mushrooms for lots of reasons. Some people look only for edible species, and use them to prepare gourmet feasts. Others enjoy the challenge of identifying all kinds of mushrooms. And some folks just love the pure beauty of mushrooms, and the pleasure of being outdoors. Many mushroom hunters start out as foragers for edible mushrooms, but then get hooked and become hunters for identification or photography. Whatever your reason for mushroom hunting, you will surely have fun!

Cantharellus lateritius, p. 102

Cliff White

Fungi and Mushrooms: What Are They?

Fungi are masses of living threads that grow underground in the soil, on leaf litter, on decaying wood and in other similar habitats. **Mushrooms** are the fruiting bodies of fungi, the parts that grow above the ground and produce **spores**.

Fungi were once considered to be in the plant kingdom, but today they are in a kingdom of their own—the Fungi. Unlike plants, fungi do not have true stems, leaves or roots, and they do not contain chlorophyll, which plants need in order to live. Instead, fungi feed on living or dead plants and animals.

A fungus begins from a spore, which germinates and sends out a network of fine, hairlike filaments. These filaments are called **hyphae**. In time, the hyphae bond together and become a dense, white, cobwebby substance that "eats" its way through the earth and all that is in the earth. This substance is called a **mycelium**. When conditions such as temperature, moisture, nutrition and light are perfect, a fruiting body, or mushroom, is formed from this mycelium. Eventually the mushroom will release spores, which are carried by wind and water to new locations.

Fungi can be saprophytic, parasitic or mycorrhizal. **Saprophytic** fungi live on organic matter that is already dead, like stumps, leaves, twigs and logs. Saprophytic fungi are what make living matter in the woods eventually break down into humus, which enriches the

The principal parts of a mushroom

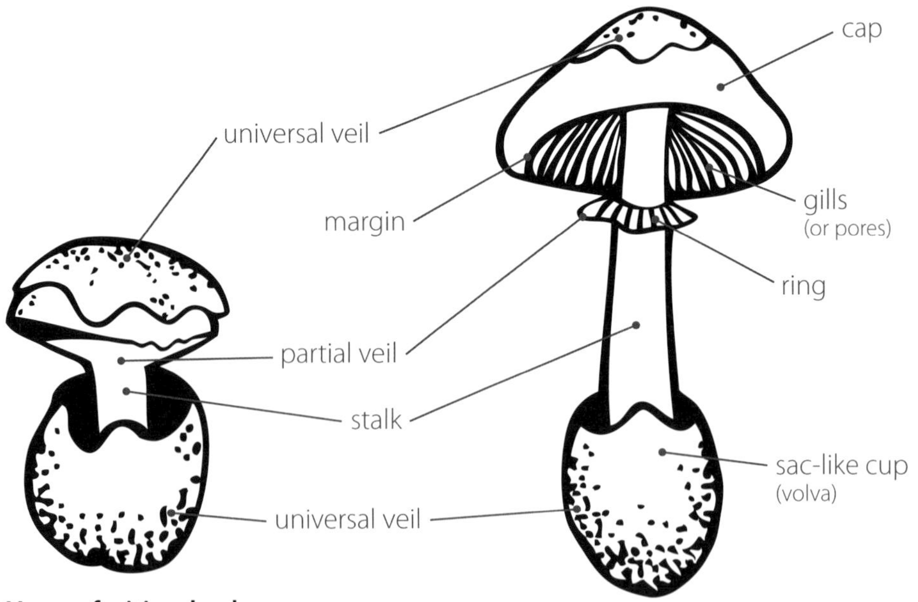

Young fruiting body (just out of the egg stage)

Mature fruiting body

soil. It takes about 20 years for a medium-sized dead oak tree to completely decay back into the earth. If there were no saprophytic fungi, plants, trees and some animals would never decompose.

Parasitic fungi feed on plants and animals that are still alive. The organism that is parasitized by a fungus is called its **host**. A parasitic fungus takes nutrition from its living host and thrives at its expense. The host is weakened by the fungal infection and eventually may die.

Mycorrhizal fungi live on certain plants in ways that help both partners. The fungus supplies the plant with water, nitrogen, and minerals, and the plant supplies the fungus with carbon from photosynthesis. They work in harmony, each benefiting from the other's offerings. This survival strategy is called **symbiosis**. Many fungi are symbiotic with trees, especially oaks, elms and pines.

Fungi and their fruiting bodies, mushrooms, are part of our natural environment. Their importance in forest ecosystems is monumental. Besides nourishing forest trees through symbiosis, they are also the wood rotters of the natural world. Fungi start the decay, then insects, bacteria and microscopic life forms continue the process, transforming wood and leaves into rich forest soil. Without fungi, forests could not exist. Isn't nature remarkable?

Patrick Harvey

Bondarzewia berkeleyi, p. 94

How to Mushroom Hunt

Missouri is a great place to find all kinds of wild mushrooms. Our state has the right climate and habitats for growing dozens of good edible mushroom species, as well as two groups of highly prized edibles—the morels and chanterelles. Missourians can also enjoy hunting for a wonderful variety of non-edible mushrooms.

Cliff White

Cantharellus lateritius, p. 102

When and Where to Find Mushrooms

Between late March and early November, after a few good rainy days, go out and see what you can find. Look in Missouri woodlands, especially those with older trees. Check out moist, timbered slopes, rich bottomlands, pastures, meadows and old orchards. (Be sure to ask permission if you don't own the land.) Or you can stay close to home, and check out mulch piles, grass, tree stumps, disturbed areas, and garden beds. In the right weather, mushrooms can grow just about anywhere!

To help you locate specific mushrooms, each of the species descriptions in this book includes the season and habitat in which that mushroom is found. If you'd like some expert guidance, you might try going on a foray with the Missouri Mycological Society (see p. 17). It's an excellent way to learn to identify mushrooms and have lots of fun while you do.

Getting Ready

Mushroom hunting is a simple and inexpensive hobby. Here are a few tips that can help you prepare and make your time more enjoyable.

Bugs

We all know that bugs are part of nature and are on this beautiful earth for a reason. However, you and I also know that they can be pesky and annoying and leave a good itch. In the Missouri woods, mosquitoes hover, ticks abound and chiggers are insidious. Before you head out to hunt mushrooms, remember to protect yourself from these pests.

Since we often go off the trail when mushroom hunting, long pants are a must. A long-sleeved, lightweight shirt is also a good idea. Many people tuck their pants legs into their socks, then dust their legs with sulfur powder, purchased at a pharmacy. This is supposed to keep the chiggers and ticks out. (However, I got my very worst case of chiggers many years ago when I used this technique. I leave this decision up to you.)

Spray yourself with a good bug spray. I use one with 15–25% DEET, or a citronella or eucalyptus spray. I've heard that a rub of catnip works well. Eating garlic and/or taking Vitamin B-6 the day before might also provide protection. You can also treat your clothes with a spray that has permethrin in it. (Be sure to follow the instructions, since permethrin is toxic.)

Equipment

The equipment you need for mushroom hunting is quite simple. All that's really required is a basket and a knife. A flat-bottomed basket is an excellent container for mushrooms. Bring one that has a somewhat tight weave. This will let air in and mushrooms spores out, yet your mushrooms will not fall through. Your knife should have a rather wide blade, so that you can dig mushrooms out of soil or wood. (A locking blade is best, so it doesn't accidentally close on your finger!)

Other items that might be helpful when mushroom hunting are: a water bottle for hydration, a compass to help you figure out where you are, wax bags (not plastic) for fragile or suspicious-looking finds, a magnifying lens to look closely at parts of mushrooms, a pen and paper to take notes, and a couple of good field guides for proper identification.

The Hunt Is On

When you are out in the woods and fields, use your "mushroom eyes." Go slowly and focus on details. Look closely at the ground, and at fallen logs and branches.

Johann Bruhn

Tylopilus felleus, p. 71

If you find a mushroom that you would like to identify, dig it out of its **substrate** so that nothing is broken, making sure the entire stalk is intact. Sometimes part of the stalk, which may include a cup or bulb, is hidden below the ground, so be gentle and careful when digging. You may even want to take some of the substrate with you in order to make identification easier. Put the mushroom in your basket, or in a wax paper bag if it is fragile, and take it with you for later identification. (Plastic doesn't work as it keeps in too much moisture and your mushrooms will deteriorate quickly.)

It's a good idea to take field notes when you collect a mushroom. Our memories aren't always perfect! Some details that can be helpful include:

- The material on which the mushroom is growing (dead or living wood, leaf litter, soil, moss)
- Whether the mushroom is single, part of a cluster, or in a scattered group
- The color of the cap, gills and stem when fresh
- Any other distinctive features, such as an odor, or a color change when bruised
- Nearby trees (elms, oaks) on which the mushroom might be mycorrhizal

If you see a large patch of edible mushrooms, take a deep breath and relax. Then decide for what purpose you want these mushrooms. Please, take only as much as you will eat. Areas have been stripped from too much mushroom hunting. (See Ethics of Mushroom Hunting, page 11)

After the Hunt

Maxine Stone

So you have a basket overflowing with mushrooms, and are tired but happy after a great day of mushroom hunting. Now what?

It's best to identify your mushrooms when the specimens are fresh and spore prints are still possible. Spread the mushrooms on a table, prepare caps for spore printing (see page 23), and get out your field notes and mushroom identification guides. Keep a record of each mushroom you identify—or mark it in your field guide. Over time, you'll be surprised at how many you have been able to ID.

If you have collected some mushrooms you plan to eat, check each one carefully to confirm its identification. One Destroying Angel in a batch of innocent Meadow Mushrooms may have disastrous consequences. Throw out old or decaying specimens, pick off any moving creatures, brush off dirt (rinsing only if necessary), and store them in the refrigerator. Mushrooms should be used as soon as possible for the best results. They can also be preserved by drying or freezing. (See page 144.)

If you don't have time to identify all the mushrooms you have collected, they can be placed in paper bags and stored for a few days in the refrigerator. If you really want to know the identity of a mushroom and just can't figure it out, don't be shy about contacting an expert to help you.

Ethics of Mushroom Hunting

We see a morel, we pick a morel. We see a Meadow Mushroom, we pick a Meadow Mushroom. We see a Chicken of the Woods, we pick a Chicken of the Woods.

Wouldn't it be great if mushroom hunting were that simple? Occasionally it is. But more often, it's important to stop and think. Will picking those enticing mushrooms bother other people, or disturb the environment?

If you want to be an ethical mushroom hunter (and you do, of course!), here are some guidelines to follow.

- If you see a mushroom on someone's property and would like to take it, always ask the property owner for permission. If permission is granted, it is kind to offer the owner some of your edible finds.

- If you are in a park, ask the park attendant if it is all right to take mushrooms. Often, mushroom hunting on public land is perfectly fine. The Missouri Department of Conservation and Missouri Department of Natural Resources have been very generous in allowing mushroom hunting. But please check it out—*before* you hunt.

- Be careful where you step. Watch out for critters, flowers, animal homes and yes, even spider webs. You won't want to damage the natural area around you.

- If you see a "mess" of edible mushrooms, please don't take them all. Leave small mushrooms, and damaged or otherwise imperfect mushrooms. It is best to take only what you can consume in the next day or two and not take every mushroom in sight. Taking everything could mean far fewer spores produced this season, and smaller mushroom crops in coming years.

- When hunting for non-edible mushrooms, try to take only one or two of each specimen for identification purposes. There is no need to take more. In this way you will disturb nature as little as possible.

- Use a basket or a mesh bag to hold your finds. The spores of the mushrooms will go through the openings and fall to the earth—where they can germinate, form a mycelium, and produce more mushrooms.

Now go find those fungi…

Maxine Stone

Guidelines for Collecting Edible Wild Mushrooms

"There are old mushroom hunters, and there are bold mushroom hunters, but there are NO old, bold mushroom hunters." This is a common and wise adage one hears when first learning how to find edible mushrooms. Listen to it carefully.

I don't want to scare anyone, but please don't eat a mushroom unless you are 100% sure of its identification. I strongly recommend that beginning collectors consult a mushroom expert before eating any wild mushroom.

The table on page 14 lists the four common deadly mushrooms described in this book. ***Learn these mushrooms well!*** Also, take careful note of the five mushrooms that are listed as poisonous, so you can avoid putting them in your "edibles" basket. Then you can concentrate on collecting mushrooms that are edible, good, excellent and CHOICE.

Please remember, however, that this book does not contain every poisonous mushroom species found in Missouri—just the most common ones. Even if your mushroom doesn't look like any of the poisonous species in this book, *you still must match it to a description of an edible species before you can consider eating it.*

Here are a few more important things to remember when collecting (and preparing) edible wild mushrooms.

- When you have found a good number of edible mushrooms, go through them to make sure that each and every one is what you think it is. It's very easy to slip in a few that look similar to your edible collection, but are actually different species. This can be dangerous!
- Please don't collect mushrooms that might be contaminated with pesticides. Don't hunt near railroad tracks, as these areas are heavily sprayed. Golf courses are also places that get a lot of pesticides. Even lawns that have been chemically treated are not good places to pick your mushrooms.
- A word to people from other countries. You may find mushrooms in Missouri that you think look "exactly like" the edible ones you find back home. Be careful! They actually may be poisonous "look-alikes" that grow here but not in your native country. Mistaking similar-looking mushrooms is the #1 cause of mushroom poisoning in the United States. Check with someone who is familiar with Missouri mushrooms before eating any tempting look-alikes.
- Wild mushrooms should never be eaten raw. Raw mushrooms are difficult to digest, and also could contain toxins or contaminants which are destroyed by cooking.
- The first time you eat any wild mushroom, put a few aside in the refrigerator. If someone has an allergic or poisonous reaction, an expert can use these samples to make a clear identification and the correct remedy can be given. (Please do this even if you are positive you have an edible species. Some people are allergic to mushrooms that other people can eat without a problem.)

David Stonner

Laccaria ochropurpurea, p. 32

Common Poisonous Mushrooms in Missouri

The following mushrooms in this book* are considered DEADLY:

Common name	Latin name	Page
Destroying Angel	*Amanita bisporigera*	39
Deadly Galerina	*Galerina autumnalis*	47
Gabled False Morel	*Gyromitra brunnea*	106
Big Red False Morel	*Gyromitra caroliniana*	107

The following mushrooms in this book* could make you sick:

Common name	Latin name	Page
Green-spored Lepiota	*Chlorophyllum molybdites*	46
Big Laughing Gym	*Gymnopilus junonius*	48
Jack O'Lantern	*Omphalotus illudens*	34
Emetic Russula	*Russula emetica*	36
Pigskin Puffball	*Scleroderma citrinum*	117

* This book includes Missouri's *most common* poisonous mushrooms, but may not include *every* poisonous mushroom in the state.

Amanita bisporigera, p. 39

Galerina autumnalis, p. 47

Russula emetica, p. 36

When thinking about collecting a batch of mushrooms, try to remember these **simple rhymes:**

When in doubt,
Throw it out!

Raw is bad,
Yes, you've been had.

If it's little and brown
It could put you down.

If the mushroom's all white
You could die, that's right!

One hundred percent is the only ID
Ninety-nine's not enough for you and me.

Amanitas are nice
But it's a roll of the dice.

Morels are great
But the false we hate.

Pores of red
May put you to bed.

Bruising blue
Is not for you.

Save a bit for the doc
In case of shock.

False Morels—Poisonous or Not?

False morels are most definitely ***poisonous*** mushrooms. The poison in false morels (*Gyromitra spp.*) is a substance called gyromitrin. This compound is metabolized in the body to monomethylhydrazine (MMH), a chemical which is used in rocket fuel. Symptoms of *Gyromitra* poisoning include nausea, vomiting, diarrhea, and in rare cases convulsions, coma and death.

Some people try to avoid poisoning by twice parboiling the mushrooms, leaving the lid off to evaporate the MMH. However, this volatile chemical can still be inhaled. The danger from standing near a boiling pot, and from eating the cooked mushroom without knowing if all of the MMH has been evaporated, makes any false morel a mushroom you shouldn't eat!

Gyromitra caroliniana, p. 107

Kids and Mushrooms

Jon Rapp

Kids are natural mushroom hunters. They are curious, energetic and love to romp in the woods. You and your kids may want to search for a specific mushroom, like morels or chanterelles. Or you may want to go out and just see what is there. Mushroom hunting is great fun for adults and children alike.

If you are looking for a specific mushroom, show your kids a picture of it before you start hunting. This will help them get those "morel eyes" or "chanterelle eyes". Once that first mushroom is found, everybody should take a good look around—there will be more!

When you're in the woods looking for mushrooms, expect the unexpected. Look in unusual places—under logs, in cracks of trees, on branches. Some mushrooms are tiny; others can weigh several pounds. Some have strange shapes; many are absolutely gorgeous. Let your children take a sample of each species they find.

After the hunt, you may want to use a field guide to identify what you have found. If your child doesn't want to do this with you, that's OK. Sometimes just the hunt is what he or she finds interesting, but some children want to learn more. Follow the lead of your kids and always keep it fun—and positive.

Once you are home, you may want to make a spore print of a mushroom that you've collected. (See Making a Spore Print, page 23.) Not only is this a fun activity for kids (and adults), it's also an excellent way to get an accurate identification of a mushroom.

Children in most European countries, especially in Eastern Europe, become mushroom hunters at an early age. It's part of family life. They forage for dinner. They forage for fun. Often they know many edible mushrooms before they are teenagers, and delight in bringing home their finds. These children never hear adults referring to mushrooms as slimy, nasty, dangerous or dirty. Mushroom hunting is in their bones and part of their heritage.

People in the United States, however, have become a bit obsessed with health and cleanliness. As a result, many of our children have become removed from the natural world. It's very important for kids to feel safe outdoors, and comfortable in the woods. Please be assured that touching mushrooms—even poisonous mushrooms—will not hurt you or your child. Actually, there are very few deadly poisonous mushrooms, and to be harmful they have to be ingested.

Don't be afraid to take your children out for a good mushroom hunt. If you want to eat some mushrooms and don't know what they are, call an expert. The success of a fun foray and a tempting table will leave your kids, and you, wanting more.

Introduction to the Missouri Mycological Society

The purpose of the Missouri Mycological Society (MOMS) is to:

- foster and expand the understanding of mushrooming
- promote the hunting and identification of wild mushrooms
- provide opportunities to share ideas, experiences and knowledge about mushroom hunting in Missouri

MOMS began in 1987. It is one of about 100 amateur mushrooms clubs affiliated with the North American Mycological Association (NAMA). MOMS offers forays, events, classes, research opportunities and much learning and fun for all members.

MOMS does not have regular meetings. Instead, it holds forays and other gatherings. When a foray takes place, we meet at a selected area and spend a couple of hours hunting and collecting mushrooms. We then gather to identify what we have found.

MOMS also has a number of weekend events throughout the year, like Morel Madness (held every year in April), Sweat 'n Chanterelles, "Mingo," and The Hawnting. For an entire weekend we hunt, learn from professionals, and eat well. Of course, being with other mycophiles gives everyone a special camaraderie.

Perhaps you've tasted your first morel and now want to find your own. Or you've taken an autumn walk and been amazed at the abundance of fungi and want to know more. Or you just have to know if that white mushroom in your yard is edible or poisonous! MOMS is a good way to get started. You'll get the support you need to be a smart and safe mushroom hunter.

Please visit the web site for the Missouri Mycological Society at: ***www.MoMyco.org***

Catherine Williamson

Lactarius glaucescens
poisonous
Lactarius corrugis
Amanita flavoconia
"Yellow Patches"
Mycena sp
Amanita vaginata
(complex)
"The Blusher"
American Style!
Tremellodendron pallidum
"False Jelly Coral"
Leotia lubrica
"Jelly Babies"
Lycoperdon sp.

Jon Rapp

Identification

SECTION II

Mushroom identification can be challenging—but if I can do it, you can do it!

This section contains detailed descriptions of 102 common Missouri mushrooms, divided into categories by shape and other visual features. When you have found a mushroom you would like to identify, follow the instructions on page 22.

Jon Rapp

Polyporus alveolaris, p. 79

Mushroom Groups by Shape

(and other visual features)

Shape/Feature	Mushroom Taxonomic Group(s)
Gilled Cap	Agarics (in general) pages 25–62
Standard	Agarics (with none of the features below) pages 26–38
Ringed	Most amanitas, some other agarics pages 39–50
Milky	*Lactarius* pages 51–54
Inky	*Coprinellus*, *Coprinopsis*, *Coprinus* pages 55–57
Little	*Marasmius*, *Mycena*, *Hygrocybe* pages 58–62
Pored Cap	Boletes, a few polypores pages 63–72
Pored Bracket	Most polypores pages 73–86
Single	pages 74–80
Layered	pages 81–86

Shape/Feature	Mushroom Taxonomic Group(s)
Gilled* Bracket	A few polypores, *Pleurotus* pages 87–91
Rosette	A few polypores, *Sparassis* pages 93–97
Vase	Chanterelles, *Hypomyces* pages 99–104
Club	Morels and false morels pages 105–110
Ball	Puffballs, earthstars, *Lycogala* pages 111–117
Tooth	Tooth fungi pages 119–122
Coral	Coral fungi, *Tremellodendron* pages 123–125
Column	Stinkhorns, earth tongues pages 127–130
Cup	Cup fungi, bird's-nest fungi pages 131–136
Jelly	Jelly fungi pages 137–141

* *With either true gills or gill-like structures*

How to Use this Section

- First, look closely at the shape and features of the mushroom you're trying to identify. Then, from among the icons in the table on p. 20–21, choose the one that most closely resembles your unknown mushroom.
- After you choose an icon, go to the pages listed for that icon. Browse through the photographs of mushrooms on those pages until you find one that looks like yours.
- Read the complete description of that mushroom. Compare the characteristics of your unknown mushroom with the details in the description.
    - It's important to remember that all of the visual details of your mushroom must match the species description. If the description says a mushroom species has crowded gills, and yours has distant gills, keep looking! It isn't necessary to look at the spores through a microscope; just check all of the characteristics you can see with your eyes alone, or with a hand lens.
    - Color is hard to communicate. Pictures often don't represent the exact color. Words don't do color justice. And nature is sometimes tricky. Use your best judgement when comparing the color of a mushroom to the descriptions and photos in this book.
    - If you are uncertain about the meaning of any term, look it up in the glossary.
- AND FINALLY: Before you eat any wild mushroom, have an expert confirm its identification. Instead of the edible mushroom you think you have, you may have an uncommon poisonous look-alike that is not covered in this book. Finding a mushroom expert may not be easy, but the Missouri Mycological Society (***www.MoMyco.org***) is a good place to start.

David Yates

Morchella esculenta, p. 109

Making a Spore Print

When you are trying to identify a mushroom, knowing the color of its spores is often very helpful. Fortunately, it's easy to determine spore color by taking a spore print.

First, cut or break off the stalk close to the cap of the mushroom. Place the cap, with the gills or pores facing down, on a piece of white paper. (To better see light-colored spores, you can use black paper, or two pieces of paper—one white and one black—taped together side by side.) Cover the mushroom with a glass or bowl and let it be. If your mushroom is at the right stage—not too young or too old—it will drop its spores in 2 to 24 hours. Your spore print may be a beautiful piece of art and even frameable.

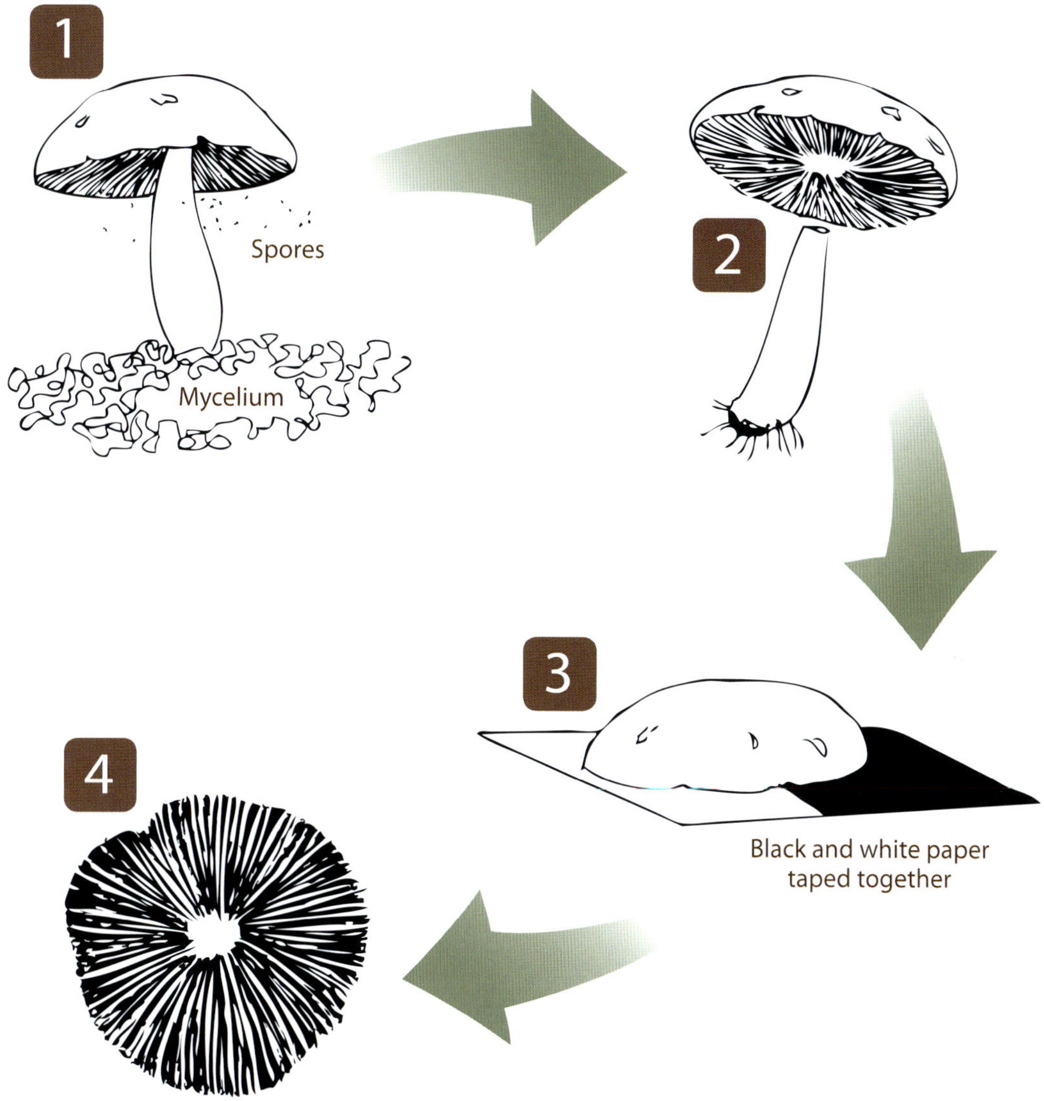

Edibility Terms and Symbols

In the mushroom species descriptions on the following pages, I have tried to be completely clear about what is and what is not an edible mushroom. The edibility status of each mushroom is indicated in two ways: by a symbol next to the "Edibility" heading, and by a term just beneath it.

Below is a list of these edibility symbols and terms. As you can see, all mushrooms with more than one star I consider pretty darn good, and there are a lot of them. Be careful and have fun.

★★★★	**CHOICE**	Absolutely delicious—the best
★★★	**Excellent**	Really, really good
★★	**Good**	Pretty good—put it in a stir fry to give it flavor
★	**Edible**	OK, you can eat it, but why?
⚠	**With caution**	This mushroom has a look-alike that is poisonous, or requires caution for some other reason
℞	**Medicinal**	This mushroom has been used for medicinal purposes
⃠	**Not recommended**	This is an edible mushroom, but it's too easily confused with a poisonous mushroom and therefore too risky
✕	**Not Edible**	Unpleasant to eat, or edibility is not known
☠	**Poisonous**	Eating this mushroom definitely causes illness
☠	**DEADLY**	Deaths from eating this mushroom have been reported

Cliff White

Lactarius volemus, p. 54

Gilled Cap

(Agarics)

Mushrooms with gilled caps are the ones that you think of when you think "mushroom." Their caps are usually circular, with blade-like gills on the underside, and in most species the stalk is attached in the center of the cap. These mushrooms are commonly called "agarics," after the taxonomic order Agaricales. Most agarics grow on the ground or on well-rotted wood. This is a large group that contains many excellent edibles and some deadly poisonous mushrooms.

For easier identification of the species in this category, I've separated out four subcategories of agarics with special visual features. These subcategories are Ringed, Milky, Inky, and Little (see below). The species descriptions are located after those of the "standard" agarics, which do not have these features. Look for the icons!

Ringed—If you have a gilled mushroom with a ring on the stalk, look under this subcategory. Most *Amanita* species have rings, as do some other agarics. However, keep in mind that rings often become fainter or disappear entirely with age. It's always a good idea to choose younger, fresher mushrooms for identification purposes.

Milky—When you run a knife or fingernail over the gills of a "milky," it will bleed a latex-like material, which may be white or colored. Bleeding will be most prolific in young specimens; old, dry specimens may not bleed at all. Milkies are in the genus *Lactarius*.

Inky—This is an interesting group. The "inkies" first appear to have a white underside, but the gills soon become gray, then black, then dissolve into a black liquid. If you see a mushroom that has a tinge of gray or black on its gills, look here. Inkies belong in the genera *Coprinellus*, *Coprinopsis* and *Coprinus*.

Little—Many agaric species are small when immature, but eventually grow to be much larger mushrooms. "Little" agarics, in contrast, never get very big. Their cap width at maturity is usually less than 2". Some of these species are very tiny and delicate, like the Orange Pinwheel Marasmius (*Marasmius siccus*, p. 60). Others, like the Fairy Ring Mushroom (*Marasmius oreades*, p. 59), are a bit sturdier, but remain small at maturity. It helps to look at specimens in different stages of growth to make sure you have a "little" mushroom.

Meadow Mushroom

(Agaricus campestris)

Michael Kuo

Smooth white to light grayish cap, pinkish-brown gills, found in lawns and meadows

Edibility ★★★★ ⚠
CHOICE—with extreme caution! The deadly Destroying Angel can grow in the same habitat as the Meadow Mushroom (see Look-alikes).

Season July–September

Habitat Scattered to abundant in grassy areas, urban lawns, meadows

Cap **Width:** 1–4″ ▪ **Shape:** Curved to nearly flat ▪ **Color:** White to grayish to gray-brown ▪ **Texture:** Dry, smooth or fibrous

Gills **Width:** Broad ▪ **Spacing:** Crowded ▪ **Color:** Light pink, becoming chocolate to blackish-brown ▪ **Attachment:** Free

Stalk **Length:** 1–2″ ▪ **Width:** $\frac{3}{8}$–$\frac{3}{4}$″ ▪ **Shape:** Sometimes tapering downward ▪ **Color:** White, darkening with age ▪ **Texture:** Smooth to fibrous ▪ **Other features:** Delicate ring that often disappears

Veil *Partial veil* white, membranous, leaving a delicate ring on the stalk

Spores **Spore print color:** Blackish-brown ▪ **Spores magnified:** Elliptical, smooth, purple-brown

Look-alikes The Destroying Angel (*Amanita bisporigera*, p. 39) has *white gills*, a *white spore print*, and a sac-like cup around the base of the stalk. The Meadow Mushroom has light pink to blackish-brown gills, and a blackish-brown spore print. (Always confirm the identification of each and every Meadow Mushroom before eating, either by making a spore print or by taking your specimens to an expert.)

The Meadow Mushroom is closely related to the cultivated, store-bought white button mushroom.

Grisette

(Amanita vaginata)

Michael Kuo

Gray cap with white patches and a radially grooved margin, stalk with a large, white, sac-like cup around the base

Edibility ⃠

Not Recommended. Although some people have been known to eat the Grisette, not enough is known about its edibility to recommend it. It could easily be mistaken for a deadly *Amanita*.

Season June–September

Habitat On the ground in open woods, and in grass near trees

Cap **Width:** 2–4″ ▪ **Shape:** Oval, becoming bell-shaped to convex or flat, with a central knob ▪ **Color:** Gray, with a few white patches ▪ **Texture:** Smooth, tacky when wet ▪ **Other features:** Margin radially grooved

Gills **Width:** Moderately broad ▪ **Spacing:** Close to distant ▪ **Color:** Whitish ▪ **Attachment:** Free

Stalk **Length:** 4–8″ ▪ **Width:** ¼–¾″ ▪ **Shape:** Cylindrical, with an elongated, white, sac-like cup around the base ▪ **Color:** Whitish ▪ **Texture:** Smooth or mealy ▪ **Other features:** Hollow, no ring

Veil *Universal veil* white, leaving patches on the cap and a large, white, sac-like cup around the base of the stalk

Spores **Spore print color:** White ▪ **Spores magnified:** Round, smooth

Look-alikes Other *Amanita* species

Recent research, including DNA testing, has shown that what we now call *Amanita vaginata* is actually many different species. In the near future taxonomists will probably divide this species and create others.

Ringless Honey Mushroom

(Armillaria tabescens)

Michael Kuo

Honey-colored, dry, scaly cap,
no ring on stalk

Edibility ★★
Good, when young and fresh. The Ringless Honey Mushroom is a good edible, but causes stomach upset in some people. Try a small amount at first and make sure it is fully cooked.

Season September–November

Habitat Clustered at bases of trees or stumps, especially oaks, and over buried wood

Cap **Width:** 1–4″ ▪ **Shape:** Convex, then flattened, margin uplifted with age ▪ **Color:** Yellow-brown to honey-brown, with reddish-brown cottony scales ▪ **Texture:** Dry, scaly

Gills **Width:** Narrow to broad ▪ **Spacing:** Distant ▪ **Color:** Whitish, staining pinkish to brownish ▪ **Attachment:** Slightly descending

Stalk **Length:** 2–8″ ▪ **Width:** ¼–½″ ▪ **Shape:** Thick, tapering toward base ▪ **Color:** Off-white to brownish ▪ **Texture:** Fibrous ▪ **Other features:** Grows in clusters with stalks fused at the base

Spores **Spore print color:** White ▪ **Spores magnified:** Elliptical, smooth, colorless

Look-alikes The Honey Mushroom (*Armillaria mellea*, p. 45) has a sticky cap and a ring. The poisonous Jack O'Lantern (*Omphalotus illudens*, p. 34) is orange and has a smooth cap. The hallucinogenic Big Laughing Gym (*Gymnopilus junonius*, p. 48) is orange, bitter and has orange-brown spores and a ring. The Deadly Galerina (*Galerina autumnalis*, p. 47) is smaller, has a smooth cap, a ring on the stalk and brown spores.

The Ringless Honey Mushroom is a parasite on living trees. It is in the same genus as the "Humongous Fungus," an *Armillaria* mycelium that is over 2.5 square miles in size! One specimen is estimated to be more than 450 years old.

Silvery-violet Cort

(Cortinarius alboviolaceus)

Dry, grayish-violet cap, pale violet gills, a club-shaped stalk and a cobwebby partial veil.

Jon Rapp

Edibility ⃠
Not Recommended. The Silvery-violet Cort could be confused with some poisonous *Cortinarius* species.

Season August–October

Habitat Single to many in mixed woods

Cap **Width:** 1¼–3″ ▪ **Shape:** Bell-shaped, with incurved margin ▪ **Color:** Grayish-violet ▪ **Texture:** Dry, silky ▪ **Other features:** On young specimens, a noticeable fine, cobwebby veil that stretches from the margin to the stalk

Gills **Width:** Broad ▪ **Spacing:** Close ▪ **Color:** Pale violet becoming rusty, cinnamon brown with age ▪ **Attachment:** Attached

Stalk **Length:** 1½–3″ ▪ **Width:** ¼–½″ ▪ **Shape:** Enlarging toward base ▪ **Color:** Violet ▪ **Texture:** Fibrous, dry

Veil *Universal veil* white, leaving a sheath-like covering on the stalk. *Partial veil* white and cobwebby.

Spores **Spore print color:** Rust ▪ **Spores magnified:** Elliptical, brownish

Look-alikes Other *Cortinarius* species, some of which are poisonous. The choice Blewit (*Lepista nuda*, p. 33) does not have a veil and the gills do not turn brown with age. The Purple-gilled Laccaria (*Laccaria ochropurpurea*, p. 32) has white to pale violet spores and no veil.

All mushrooms in the genus *Cortinarius* have a cortina (a cobwebby veil) that goes from the cap margin to the stalk but may disappear with age. All Corts have rusty brown spores that often leave the gills a rusty brown color.

Velvet Foot

(Flammulina velutipes)

Tawny, sticky cap with whitish gills; stalk yellowish above and brownish below

Brad Bomanz

Michael Kuo

Edibility ⃠

Not Recommended. Although this is an edible mushroom, I don't recommend eating the Velvet Foot as it can be easily confused with the Deadly Galerina (see Look-alikes). Since it isn't a particularly tasty mushroom anyway, don't chance it!

Season October–May

Habitat In clusters on deciduous logs

Cap **Width:** 1–2″ ▪ **Shape:** Convex to flat with knob ▪ **Color:** Tawny to reddish-brown/yellow ▪ **Texture:** Smooth, sticky to tacky to slimy

Gills **Width:** Broad ▪ **Spacing:** Fairly well separated ▪ **Color:** Whitish to yellowish ▪ **Attachment:** Notched

Stalk **Length:** 2–3″ ▪ **Width:** ⅛ – ¼″ ▪ **Shape:** Narrowing downward ▪ **Color:** Yellowish above, brownish-black below ▪ **Texture:** Velvety

Spores **Spore print color:** White ▪ **Spores magnified:** Elliptical, smooth, colorless

Look-alikes The Deadly Galerina (*Galerina autumnalis*, p. 47) has brown spores and a ring on the stalk.

Believe it or not, the wild Velvet Foot is the same mushroom as the cultivated Enoki that you can buy at Asian grocery stores. Since Enoki mushrooms are grown in jars in the dark, they have long stalks and are white in color.

Common Laccaria

(Laccaria laccata)

Small, brownish-pink cap with a central depression, and pale pinkish-brown gills and stalk

Jon Rapp

Edibility ★
Edible

Season June–November

Habitat Scattered or in groups in poor or sandy soil, in mixed woods

Cap **Width:** ½–2″ ▪ **Shape:** Convex to flat with a central depression ▪ **Color:** Brownish-pink becoming pinkish becoming off-white ▪ **Texture:** Smooth ▪ **Other features:** Margin curves in at first, becoming finely wavy

Gills **Width:** Broad ▪ **Spacing:** Distant ▪ **Color:** Pale pinkish-brown ▪ **Attachment:** Attached or slightly descending the stalk ▪ **Other features:** Thick

Stalk **Length:** 1–3″ ▪ **Width:** ⅛–½″ ▪ **Shape:** Almost equal ▪ **Color:** Light brownish to tawny to pinkish ▪ **Texture:** Tough, fibrous

Spores **Spore print color:** White ▪ **Spores magnified:** Broadly elliptical, spiny, colorless

Look-alikes Other *Laccaria* species, none of which are known to be poisonous

The Common Laccaria is often called "The Deceiver" because it is quite variable in appearance and may be difficult to distinguish from other *Laccaria* species.

Purple-gilled Laccaria

(Laccaria ochropurpurea)

David Stonner

Large, tannish-lavender cap with thick, purplish gills and a stout stalk

Edibility ★★
Good

Season July–November

Habitat Scattered or in groups in grassy areas and under oaks

Cap **Width:** 2–8″ ▪ **Shape:** Convex, becoming flat to depressed in the center ▪ **Color:** Tannish-lavender, becoming grayish-white ▪ **Texture:** Smooth ▪ **Other features:** Margin curves in at first, becoming finely wavy

Gills **Width:** Broad ▪ **Spacing:** Distant ▪ **Color:** Purplish ▪ **Attachment:** Attached ▪ **Other features:** Thick

Stalk **Length:** 2–8″ ▪ **Width:** 3/8–3/4″ ▪ **Shape:** Often curved, stout ▪ **Color:** Tannish-lavender to grayish-white ▪ **Texture:** Smooth to slightly scaly

Spores **Spore print color:** White to pale violet ▪ **Spores magnified:** Round, spiny, colorless

Look-alikes Other *Laccaria* species, none of which are known to be poisonous. The Silvery-violet Cort (*Cortinarius alboviolaceus*, p. 29) has gills that become rust-brown and a cobwebby veil.

In Missouri's oak woods, large numbers of Purple-gilled Laccaria can often be found in the fall. Though it isn't a choice edible, it's pretty good when combined with other mushrooms or strong flavors.

Blewit

(Lepista nuda)

All parts of mushroom—cap, gills and stalk—are violet to tan

Jon Rapp

Edibility ★★★★
CHOICE. Blewits are strong and delicious mushrooms. Look for them in the fall in mulch piles, and sauté them up for dinner. (For recipe, see page 146.)

Season August–October

Habitat Scattered in open areas, in mulch piles, along paths

Cap **Width:** 1½–6″ ▪ **Shape:** Convex to flat, margin inrolled at first, becoming wavy and upturned ▪ **Color:** Violet-lilac, becoming tannish ▪ **Texture:** Smooth

Gills **Width:** Broad ▪ **Spacing:** Crowded ▪ **Color:** Violet-lilac, fading to tan ▪ **Attachment:** Notched

Stalk **Length:** 1–3″ ▪ **Width:** ½–1″ ▪ **Shape:** Often bulbous toward base ▪ **Color:** Violet-tan fading to tannish-brown ▪ **Texture:** Dry, scaly ▪ **Other features:** Solid

Spores **Spore print color:** Pinkish-buff ▪ **Spores magnified:** Elliptical, smooth, colorless

Look-alikes The Silvery-violet Cort (*Cortinarius alboviolaceus*, p. 29) has a cobwebby veil when young, and gills that turn brown.

A blewit mycelium can produce several crops per season. If you find a nice batch, check that spot again later. Previously known as *Clitocybe nuda.*

Jack O' Lantern

(Omphalotus illudens)

Clustered, bright orange to yellowish-orange, with sharp-edged gills that descend the stalk

Patrick Lennon

Edibility ☠

POISONOUS. The Jack O'Lantern will make you very sick for a few days. You won't die, but you might wish you had.

Season July–October

Habitat In clusters, at the base of stumps and buried roots of oak and other deciduous wood

Cap **Width:** 2–8″ ▪ **Shape:** Convex, becoming flat to funnel shaped, sunken in center, with incurved margins ▪ **Color:** Orange to yellowish-orange ▪ **Texture:** Smooth

Gills **Width:** Narrow to broad ▪ **Spacing:** Crowded ▪ **Color:** Orange to yellowish-orange ▪ **Attachment:** Descending the stalk ▪ **Other features:** Sharp-edged

Stalk **Length:** 2–8″ ▪ **Width:** ½–¾″ ▪ **Shape:** Curved, tapering toward the base ▪ **Color:** Same color as cap but darkening toward the base ▪ **Texture:** Smooth ▪ **Other features:** Solid

Spores **Spore print color:** Cream ▪ **Spores magnified:** Round, smooth, colorless

Look-alikes Two delicious chanterelles (*Cantharellus lateritius*, p. 102 and *C. cibarius*, p. 100) are similar in color and shape, but their undersides are smooth or have blunt ridges, not gills. They also grow singly on the forest floor and not in clusters on wood. The Honey Mushroom (*Armillaria mellea*, p. 45) and Ringless Honey Mushroom (*Armillaria tabescens*, p. 28) are honey-colored. The Big Laughing Gym (*Gymnopilus junonius*, p. 48) has orange- to rust-colored spores.

The Jack O'Lantern is bioluminescent. If you find a fresh cluster, take it into a completely dark room so you can see the eerie, greenish-yellow glow of the gills. Previously called *Omphalotus olearius.*

Fawn Mushroom

(Pluteus atricapillus)

Cliff White

Brownish-gray cap with whitish-pinkish gills and whitish stalk

Edibility ★ ⚠
Edible—with caution

Season May–October

Habitat Single or scattered, on dead wood or on the ground over buried wood

Cap **Width:** 1¼–5″ ▪ **Shape:** Convex to flat ▪ **Color:** Brownish-gray to dark brown, with darker fibers radiating from center ▪ **Texture:** Smooth, tacky when wet

Gills **Width:** Broad ▪ **Spacing:** Close ▪ **Color:** White, becoming salmon-pink ▪ **Attachment:** Free

Stalk **Length:** 2–4″ ▪ **Width:** ¼–½″ ▪ **Shape:** May enlarge slightly toward the base, straight but sometimes curved ▪ **Color:** White, can be tinged with black or brown ▪ **Texture:** Smooth with small fibers ▪ **Other features:** Solid

Spores **Spore print color:** Salmon to brownish-pink ▪ **Spores magnified:** Elliptical, smooth

Look-alikes A lot of other brownish-gray mushrooms, some of which may be poisonous

The Fawn Mushroom is a common and edible mushroom, but I don't think the flavor is one of the best and it's good only when very young. Previously called *Pluteus cervinus.*

Emetic Russula

(Russula emetica)

Jon Rapp

Uniformly red cap with off-white gills and stalk; flesh and stalk are brittle

Edibility

POISONOUS. The Emetic Russula is considered a poisonous mushroom because, as its name suggests, it will cause vomiting. The taste is very hot, spicy and acrid so it isn't appealing anyway.

Season July–October

Habitat Singly or in groups, on moss and in mixed woods

Cap **Width:** 1–4" ▪ **Shape:** Cushion-shaped, becoming convex, then becoming vase-shaped; margin is incurved ▪ **Color:** Uniformly red ▪ **Texture:** Sticky, smooth ▪ **Other features:** Flesh is white and brittle

Gills **Width:** Broad ▪ **Spacing:** Close ▪ **Color:** White, becoming off-white ▪ **Attachment:** Attached

Stalk **Length:** 2–4" ▪ **Width:** ¼–1" ▪ **Shape:** Straight, enlarging a bit at the base ▪ **Color:** Off-white ▪ **Texture:** Wrinkled ▪ **Other features:** Brittle

Spores **Spore print color:** White ▪ **Spores magnified:** Elliptical to oval, ornamented

Look-alikes There are many, many Russulas and many red Russulas. It is often difficult to tell one from another.

You can identify the genus *Russula* by its blocky shape and by the fact that Russulas are very brittle mushrooms. They will break apart in your hand like a piece of chalk. The stalk even looks like a piece of chalk.

Green Cracking Russula

(Russula virescens)

Jon Rapp

Cap with greenish, cracked, mosaic-like top, and cream gills

Edibility ★★★
Excellent. This is a very good edible mushroom.

Season July–September

Habitat Singly or in groups, in mixed woods

Cap **Width:** 2–5″ ▪ **Shape:** Cushion-shaped, becoming convex, then becoming vase-shaped; margin is incurved ▪ **Color:** Dull greenish-olive ▪ **Texture:** Surface is patched or mosaic-like ▪ **Other features:** Flesh is thick and brittle

Gills **Width:** Broad ▪ **Spacing:** Close ▪ **Color:** Cream ▪ **Attachment:** Attached

Stalk **Length:** 1½–3½″ ▪ **Width:** ¾–1½″ ▪ **Shape:** Straight ▪ **Color:** White, turning brownish ▪ **Texture:** Brittle

Spores **Spore print color:** White ▪ **Spores magnified:** Elliptical to oval, ornamented

Look-alikes There are many green Russulas, and it is often difficult to tell one from another. None of them are poisonous, though some may not taste very good. The mosaic-like, cracked pattern on the top of the Green Cracking Russula distinguishes it from other green Russulas.

Russulas are common and colorful mushrooms. You often can find them even when the woods are fairly dry.

Rooted Collybia

(Xerula radicata)

Tim Gleason

Grayish-brown, flat cap with long, slender stalk that tapers under the soil

Edibility ★★
Good

Season July–October

Habitat Single or scattered on and around deciduous trees and stumps

Cap **Width:** 1–4″ ▪ **Shape:** Slightly convex, becoming flat, with a knob in the center ▪ **Color:** Grayish-brown to dark brown; center knob is darker ▪ **Texture:** Tacky or moist

Gills **Width:** Broad ▪ **Spacing:** Distant ▪ **Color:** White ▪ **Attachment:** Attached

Stalk **Length:** 2–8″ ▪ **Width:** ⅛–⅜″ ▪ **Shape:** Enlarging toward the soil line; continues root-like under the soil and tapers to a point ▪ **Color:** Whitish above the soil, brownish below ▪ **Texture:** Snaps when broken

Spores **Spore print color:** White ▪ **Spores magnified:** Smooth, colorless, elliptical

Look-alikes Other brownish mushrooms, but this one has a "root"

The cap of the Rooted Collybia is a meaty and fairly tasty addition to your edible collection.

Previously known as *Collybia radicata* and *Oudemansiella radicata.* Actually this mushroom is a taxonomic dilemma. Research continues, as do name changes. There are many *Xerula* species, and proper identification really depends on microscopic examination.

Destroying Angel

(Amanita bisporigera)

David Stonner

All white, with a ring on the stalk and a large, sac-like cup around the base of the stalk

Edibility

DEADLY. The name "Destroying Angel" is well-deserved. Symptoms of poisoning often don't appear until 6–24 hours after eating, and include vomiting, diarrhea, and cramps. Later, kidney or liver dysfunction occurs and can lead to death.

Season June–November

Habitat Very common, on the ground in mixed woods and in grass near trees

Cap **Width:** 2–5″ ▪ **Shape:** Curved to flat with central swelling, smooth margin ▪ **Color:** dull to shiny white ▪ **Texture:** Smooth, tacky when wet

Gills **Width:** Narrow to moderately broad ▪ **Spacing:** Close ▪ **Color:** White ▪ **Attachment:** Free or slightly attached

Stalk **Length:** 3–8″ ▪ **Width:** ¼–¾″ ▪ **Shape:** Sometimes enlarging toward the base ▪ **Color:** White ▪ **Texture:** Cottony to shaggy ▪ **Other features:** A ring, and a sac-like cup around the base that may be hidden underground

Veil *Universal veil* white, leaving a large, sac-like cup around the base of the stalk and a large, white, skirt-like ring on the upper part of the stalk

Spores **Spore print color:** White ▪ **Spores magnified:** Nearly round to round, smooth

Look-alikes The edible Meadow Mushroom has pink gills which turn brown, and a brown spore print. It does not have a sac-like cup around the base. Other *Amanita* species, both harmless and poisonous, are similar in appearance to the Destroying Angel. In the past, *Amanita virosa* was considered a very close look-alike to *Amanita bisporigera*, but DNA testing has shown that *A. virosa* is not found in the United States.

The Destroying Angel is a beautiful mushroom and very common in Missouri woods. Look, but don't taste!

Citron Amanita

(Amanita citrina)

Jon Rapp

Yellowish-white cap, stalk with a ring and a bulbous, soft base

Edibility ⃠
Not Recommended. Though the Citron Amanita is not known to be poisonous, it is not recommended as an edible because it can be confused with the deadly Destroying Angel (*Amanita bisporigera*, p. 39).

Season July–November

Habitat On the ground in oak and pine woods

Cap **Width:** 2–4″ ▪ **Shape:** Convex, becoming flat ▪ **Color:** Light lemon-yellow to light greenish-yellow, with whitish patches ▪ **Texture:** Sticky when wet

Gills **Width:** Broad ▪ **Spacing:** Close ▪ **Color:** Off-white ▪ **Attachment:** Free or slightly attached

Stalk **Length:** 3–5″ ▪ **Width:** ½–¾″ ▪ **Shape:** Large, with soft bulbous base ▪ **Color:** White ▪ **Texture:** Smooth to scruffy ▪ **Other features:** Ring

Veil *Universal veil* whitish to buff, often leaving whitish patches on the cap. *Partial veil* membranous, leaving a skirt-like ring on the stalk.

Spores **Spore print color:** White ▪ **Spores magnified:** Round, smooth

Look-alikes Other *Amanita* species

The gills of the Citron Amanita smell like raw potatoes, and this odor can help with identification. However, keep in mind that other *Amanita* species not in this book may have this odor and a similar color.

Yellow Patches

(Amanita flavoconia)

Orange to yellow cap with yellowish patches, and a stalk with crumbling patches and a ring

David Stonner

Edibility ✕

Not Edible. The edibility of the Yellow Patches has not been established. It should not be eaten because it resembles other *Amanita* species, some of which are deadly.

Season June–November

Habitat On the ground in mixed woods

Cap **Width:** 1–3″ ▪ **Shape:** Convex to almost flat, with a central knob ▪ **Color:** Bright orange to yellow with yellow patches ▪ **Texture:** Sticky, smooth

Gills **Width:** Broad ▪ **Spacing:** Close ▪ **Color:** Whitish to yellowish ▪ **Attachment:** Free or slightly attached

Stalk **Length:** 2–4″ ▪ **Width:** ¼–¾″ ▪ **Shape:** Thick, with large bulb at base ▪ **Color:** White to pale yellow ▪ **Texture:** Smooth to scruffy (with crumbling patches) ▪ **Other features:** Ring

Veil *Universal veil* yellow, leaving yellow patches on the cap and crumbly remnants around the base of the stalk. *Partial veil* white to yellow, leaving a skirt-like ring on the upper stalk.

Spores **Spore print color:** White ▪ **Spores magnified:** Elliptical, smooth

Look-alikes Other *Amanita* species.

This is a very common and quite beautiful mushroom—but it's still an Amanita, so beware!

Onusta Amanita

(Amanita onusta)

Cliff White

Grayish-white cap with grayish-brown warts that are often erect, and a long stalk with grayish-brown warts

Edibility ✕
Not Edible

Season August–September

Habitat On the ground in mixed woods

Cap **Width:** 1–4″ ▪ **Shape:** Convex to almost flat, with a central knob ▪ **Color:** Grayish-white, with grayish-brown warts ▪ **Texture:** Slightly sticky when wet; warts are often erect

Gills **Width:** Medium broad ▪ **Spacing:** Close ▪ **Color:** Whitish to cream ▪ **Attachment:** Free or slightly attached

Stalk **Length:** 1½–6″ ▪ **Width:** ½–¾″ ▪ **Shape:** With bulb at base, then tapering and rooting ▪ **Color:** Grayish-white, with grayish-brown warts ▪ **Texture:** Warts on lower part ▪ **Other features:** Ring

Veil *Universal veil* whitish, leaving grayish-brown warts on the cap and stem. *Partial veil* whitish-cream, leaving a skirt-like ring on the upper stalk.

Spores **Spore print color:** White ▪ **Spores magnified:** Broadly ellipsoid

Look-alikes Other *Amanita* species. The Old Man of the Woods (*Strobilomyces floccopus*, p. 70) and the Confusing Old Man of the Woods (*Strobilomyces confusus*, p. 70) are similar in appearance, but have pores, not gills.

The Onusta Amanita is unusual in that it is a grayish-white mushroom with grayish-brown warts.

Blusher

(Amanita rubescens)

Reddish to brownish cap with pinkish-brown patches and a ring on the stalk, entire mushroom bruising reddish

David Stonner

Edibility ⃠

Not Recommended. Though this is considered an edible mushroom, it could easily be mistaken for one of the deadly *Amanita* species.

Season June–October

Habitat On the ground in oak woods and under white pines

Cap **Width:** 2–6″ ▪ **Shape:** Convex to almost flat, with a central knob ▪ **Color:** Reddish-brown with pinkish-brown patches, bruising reddish ▪ **Texture:** Smooth with cottony patches, slightly tacky when wet

Gills **Width:** Moderately broad ▪ **Spacing:** Close to crowded ▪ **Color:** Whitish, bruising reddish to reddish-brown, often quickly ▪ **Attachment:** Free or slightly attached

Stalk **Length:** 3–8″ ▪ **Width:** ¼–¾″ ▪ **Shape:** Enlarges toward the base, which is large, soft and bulbous ▪ **Color:** Whitish, bruising pink to red ▪ **Texture:** Smooth to fibrous ▪ **Other features:** Ring

Veil *Universal veil* grayish to gray-pink, leaving pinkish-brown patches on the cap. *Partial veil* whitish, staining pinkish, and leaving a skirt-like ring on the upper stalk.

Spores **Spore print color:** White ▪ **Spores magnified:** Elliptical, smooth

Look-alikes Other *Amanita* species

The Blusher is a very common Missouri mushroom. However, researchers believe that what we know as *Amanita rubescens* in North America is really not the same mushroom as in other parts of the world. It will soon be given a new Latin name.

Thiers Amanita

(Amanita thiersii)

Cap and stem large, white, sticky, and shaggy

Jon Rapp

Edibility ✕
Not Edible. The edibility of the Thiers Amanita has not been established. It should not be eaten because it could be mistaken for one of the deadly *Amanita* species.

Season June–August

Habitat Lawns, pastures, prairies, often in fairy rings

Cap **Width:** 2¾–5½″ ▪ **Shape:** Oval becoming convex ▪ **Color:** White ▪ **Texture:** Sticky, shaggy

Gills **Width:** Broad ▪ **Spacing:** Crowded ▪ **Color:** Whitish-yellow ▪ **Attachment:** Free

Stalk **Length:** 3½–8″ ▪ **Width:** ⅜–1″ ▪ **Shape:** Slightly bulbous at the base ▪ **Color:** White ▪ **Texture:** Sticky, shaggy ▪ **Other features:** Ring

Veil *Universal veil* white, collapsing on the stalk, leaving a cottony, sticky, shaggy substance

Spores **Spore print color:** White ▪ **Spores magnified:** Smooth, round to broadly elliptical

Look-alikes Other *Amanita* species. It also resembles the poisonous Green-spored Lepiota (*Chlorophyllum molybdites*, p. 46), which has green spores.

This mushroom was named after Dr. Harry Thiers (1919–2000) — mycologist, educator, researcher, and friend of the Missouri Mycological Society.

Honey Mushroom

(Armillaria mellea)

Jim Cooper

Honey-colored, sticky cap with black hairs over center, stalk with whitish ring

Edibility ★★

Good, when young and fresh. The Honey Mushroom is a good edible, but causes stomach upset in some individuals. The first time you eat it, try just a small amount and make sure it is cooked thoroughly.

Season August–November

Habitat Clustered at bases of trees or stumps, especially oaks, and over buried wood

Cap **Width:** 1–6″ ▪ **Shape:** Convex, then flattened and centrally depressed ▪ **Color:** Yellow to honey to rust brown ▪ **Texture:** Sticky with black hairy scales in center

Gills **Width:** Narrow to broad ▪ **Spacing:** Distant ▪ **Color:** Whitish, becoming darker with age ▪ **Attachment:** Attached or slightly descending

Stalk **Length:** 2–6″ ▪ **Width:** ¼–¾″ ▪ **Shape:** Thick ▪ **Color:** Whitish, becoming reddish-brown ▪ **Texture:** Fibrous ▪ **Other features:** Ring on upper stalk; grows in clusters with stalks fused at the base

Veil *Partial veil* leaving a whitish ring on stalk

Spores **Spore print color:** White ▪ **Spores magnified:** Elliptical, smooth, colorless

Look-alikes The Ringless Honey (*Armillaria tabescens*, p. 28) has a dry cap and no ring. The poisonous Jack O'Lantern (*Omphalotus illudens*, p. 34) is orange. The hallucinogenic Big Laughing Gym (*Gymnopilus junonius*, p. 48) is orange, bitter, and has orange-brown spores. The Deadly Galerina (*Galerina autumnalis*, p. 47) is smaller and has a smooth cap and brown spores.

The parasitic Honey Mushroom produces long, black, string-like cords, or **rhizomorphs**, found under the bark of trees or in the soil. These rhizomorphs can travel long distances, and produce mushrooms far from the original infected tree.

Green-spored Lepiota

(Chlorophyllum molybdites)

Gordon Maupin

Large, white, with broad, cream-colored scales on the cap, white gills that turn gray-green, and a ring on the stalk

Edibility POISONOUS

Season July–September

Habitat In lawns and meadows, often in fairy rings

Cap **Width:** 2–12″ ▪ **Shape:** Round, becoming flat ▪ **Color:** White, with large whitish, pinkish, or cream-colored patches in center ▪ **Texture:** Patches breaking into many small scales when open

Gills **Width:** Broad ▪ **Spacing:** Close ▪ **Color:** White, becoming gray-green or darker ▪ **Attachment:** Free

Stalk **Length:** 3–10″ ▪ **Width:** ¼ –1″ ▪ **Shape:** Enlarges toward the base ▪ **Color:** White, darkens when handled ▪ **Texture:** Smooth ▪ **Other features:** Ring on upper stalk

Veil *Partial veil*, leaving a ring on the stalk reminiscent of a napkin ring

Spores **Spore print color:** Green ▪ **Spores magnified:** Elliptical, smooth, with small pore at tip

Look-alikes Most *Lepiota* species have white spore prints. The Reddening Lepiota (*Lepiota americana*, p. 49) bruises red. The Parasol (*Macrolepiota procera*, p. 50) has a tall, slender, scaly stalk. The *Agaricus* species, some of which are edible—including the Meadow Mushroom (*Agaricus campestris*, p. 26)—have brown spore prints. The Thiers Amanita (*Amanita thiersii*, p. 44) has a white spore print. The Shaggy Mane (*Coprinus comatus*, p. 57) has a cylindrical cap that turns inky with age, and black spores.

The very common Green-spored Lepiota is not deadly, but it can make you sick, causing anything from a mild stomach-ache to serious illness and violent vomiting.

Deadly Galerina

(Galerina autumnalis)

Michael Kuo

Brownish, sticky cap, yellowish to rust gills, with a ring on the stalk

Edibility

DEADLY. Symptoms can begin 10 or more hours after eating. The first symptoms are vomiting, diarrhea and cramps; these may subside for a while, but later kidney or liver dysfunction can occur, and possibly death.

Season September–November

Habitat Scattered or clustered on deciduous and coniferous logs

Cap **Width:** 1–2½″ ▪ **Shape:** Convex becoming flatter ▪ **Color:** Dark brown to tawny-ochre, fading lighter ▪ **Texture:** Sticky, smooth

Gills **Width:** Broad ▪ **Color:** Yellowish becoming rust ▪ **Spacing:** Close ▪ **Attachment:** Attached

Stalk **Length:** 1–4″ ▪ **Width:** ⅛–¼″ ▪ **Shape:** Enlarging downward ▪ **Color:** Off-white above, brownish-black below ▪ **Texture:** Smooth or finely shaggy ▪ **Other features:** Hollow, with a ring

Veil *Partial veil* white, leaving a ring on upper stalk

Spores **Spore print color:** Rust ▪ **Spores magnified:** Elliptical, roughened, with slight depression

Look-alikes The Velvet Foot (*Flammulina velutipes*, p. 30) does not have a ring and has white spores. The Honey Mushroom (*Armillaria mellea*, p. 45) and the Ringless Honey Mushroom (*Armillaria tabescens*, p. 28) have white spores.

This is a very poisonous and common mushroom in the LBM (Little Brown Mushroom) category. Don't eat LBMs!

Big Laughing Gym

(Gymnopilus junonius)

Large, orangish-yellow, in clusters, with a ring on the stalk

Brad Bomanz

Edibility

POISONOUS. "In Japan this species was named the Big Laughing Gym because its ingestion has caused unmotivated laughter and foolish behavior." That being said, this mushroom has also been known to cause serious illness.

Season August–October

Habitat In clusters on stumps and trunks of deciduous trees, on the ground, or over buried wood

Cap **Width:** 3–7″ ▪ **Shape:** Convex ▪ **Color:** Orangish-yellow to fawn ▪ **Texture:** Smooth with minute scales

Gills **Width:** Broad ▪ **Color:** Light yellow to rust ▪ **Spacing:** Crowded ▪ **Attachment:** Attached

Stalk **Length:** 2–8″ ▪ **Width:** ¼–1½″ ▪ **Shape:** Equal or club-shaped ▪ **Color:** Light yellow to ochre ▪ **Texture:** Covered with tiny fibers ▪ **Other features:** Ring

Veil *Partial veil* thin and fibrous, pale yellow, leaving a line or zone on the stalk

Spores **Spore print color:** Orange to rust ▪ **Spores magnified:** Oval to elliptical, wrinkled

Look-alikes The edible Honey Mushroom (*Armillaria mellea*, p. 45) is honey-colored and has a white spore print. The edible Ringless Honey Mushroom (*Armillaria tabescens*, p. 28) is honey-colored, has a white spore print, and has no ring. The poisonous Jack O'Lantern (*Omphalotus illudens*, p. 34) does not have a veil and has a whitish-cream spore print. The extremely toxic Deadly Galerina (*Galerina autumnalis*, p. 47) is smaller and browner.

The odor of this mushroom is like anise and the taste is bitter. Previously called *Gymnopilus spectabilis*.

Reddening Lepiota

(Lepiota americana)

Michael Kuo

Large, reddish-brown mushroom with a scaly cap and a ring on the stalk; bruises dark red

Edibility ★★ ⚠
Good—with caution. Don't confuse this with the poisonous Green-spored Lepiota (see Look-alikes). Better take a spore print before eating.

Season June–October

Habitat Single or in clusters in mulch piles, waste areas, around stumps

Cap **Width:** 1–6″ ▪ **Shape:** Convex to flat, with a definite knob in the center ▪ **Color:** Whitish with pinkish scales when young, ages reddish brown; bruises dark red; flesh is white, bruising yellowish-orange when young, red with handling or with age ▪ **Texture:** Scaly

Gills **Width:** Broad ▪ **Spacing:** Close ▪ **Color:** White, turning reddish ▪ **Attachment:** Free

Stalk **Length:** 3–5″ ▪ **Width:** ¼–¾″ at the top ▪ **Shape:** Widening toward the middle, then tapering toward the bottom ▪ **Color:** White at first, staining reddish-brown with handling or age ▪ **Texture:** Smooth ▪ **Other features:** Ring

Veil *Partial veil* leaving a white, skirt-like ring on the upper stalk

Spores **Spore print color:** White ▪ **Spores magnified:** Elliptical, smooth, colorless, with a pore at the tip

Look-alikes The poisonous Green-spored Lepiota (*Chlorophyllum molybdites*, p. 46) has white gills that turn grayish-greenish, green spores, and it does not bruise red. The edible Parasol (*Macrolepiota procera*, p. 50) does not bruise red and has a scaly stalk.

The Reddening Lepiota can often be found in large groups, enough to make a good dinner.

Parasol

(Macrolepiota procera)

Michael Kuo

Very tall, cap buff to brown, broad, scaly, with a knob in center and a moveable ring on stalk

Edibility ★★★★ ⚠

CHOICE—with caution. Don't confuse this with the poisonous Green-spored Lepiota (see Look-alikes). Take a spore print before eating. (For recipe, see page 159.)

Season June–October

Habitat
Scattered on the ground, along trails, in open woods and old pastures

Cap
Width: 3–8″ ▪ **Shape:** Egg-shaped, becoming flat with a definite knob in the center ▪ **Color:** Pale buff to grayish-brown, covered with darker brown, shaggy scales ▪ **Texture:** Scaly

Gills
Width: Broad ▪ **Spacing:** Close ▪ **Color:** White, darkening with age ▪ **Attachment:** Free

Stalk
Length: 5–16″ ▪ **Width:** ¼–¾″ ▪ **Shape:** Tall and slender, with a bulbous base ▪ **Color:** Whitish, with small brownish scales ▪ **Texture:** Scaly ▪ **Other features:** Ring on upper part

Veil
Partial veil leaving a white, skirt-like ring on the upper stalk

Spores
Spore print color: White ▪ **Spores magnified:** Very large, broadly elliptical, colorless, with a pore at the tip

Look-alikes
The poisonous Green-spored Lepiota (*Chlorophyllum molybdites*, p. 46) has white gills that turn grayish-greenish, and a greenish spore print. The edible Reddening Lepiota (*Lepiota americana*, p. 49) bruises and ages red.

Look for the moveable, fringed ring on the Parasol's long stalk. Also known as *Lepiota procera.*

Hygrophorus Milky

(Lactarius hygrophoroides)

Maxine Stone

Velvety orangish-brown cap and stalk; white gills and flesh that exude an abundant milky white latex

Edibility ★★★★
CHOICE

Season June–September

Habitat Scattered in deciduous woods

Cap **Width:** 1½–4″ ▪ **Shape:** Convex, with incurved margin at first, becoming flat to vase-shaped ▪ **Color:** Orangish-brown ▪ **Texture:** Velvety, dry ▪ **Other features:** Flesh is white, exuding abundant, unchanging white latex

Latex White, abundant, not discoloring

Gills **Width:** Broad ▪ **Spacing:** Distant ▪ **Color:** White, becoming cream colored ▪ **Attachment:** Attached

Stalk **Length:** 1¼–2″ ▪ **Width:** ¼–½″ ▪ **Shape:** Equal ▪ **Color:** Orangish-brown, sometimes the same color as the cap ▪ **Texture:** Dry

Spores **Spore print color:** White ▪ **Spores magnified:** Elliptical, ornamented

Look-alikes The Voluminous Latex Milky (*Lactarius volemus*, p. 54) has close gills, a fish-like odor, and latex that stains brown.

Besides telling you that you have a *Lactarius*, the latex of a "milky" helps identify it to species. Latex color, odor, taste (mild, hot, sweet, bitter, acrid—try a tiny drop) and volume (abundant or not) are all important clues.

Indigo Milky

(Lactarius indigo)

Entire mushroom blueish, bleeding blue; then greenish, bruising greenish

David Stonner

Edibility ★★★
Excellent. (For recipe, see page 155.)

Season July–October

Habitat Scattered or in groups on soil in oak and pine woods

Cap
Width: 1–6″ ▪ **Shape:** Convex to sunken, with inrolled margin at first ▪ **Color:** Indigo blue when fresh, fading to pale grayish-blue with deep greenish bruises ▪ **Texture:** Sticky, smooth, zoned

Latex Deep indigo blue, becoming dark green with exposure to air

Gills
Width: Broad ▪ **Spacing:** Close ▪ **Color:** Dark blue becoming paler, staining blue-green when bruised ▪ **Attachment:** Attached

Stalk
Length: ½–3½″ ▪ **Width:** ½–1″ ▪ **Shape:** Often tapered toward base, becoming hollow with age ▪ **Color:** Indigo to silver blue ▪ **Texture:** Dry

Spores
Spore print color: Cream ▪ **Spores magnified:** Broadly elliptical to round, ornamented

Look-alikes None in Missouri

The color of this mushroom is very unusual, so when you see a blue mushroom that bleeds blue (really!), it is almost certainly an Indigo Milky.

Peppery Milky

(Lactarius piperatus)

Michael Kuo

Cap white, gills densely crowded, bleeding white and with a spicy-hot taste

Edibility ★

Edible. This is an edible mushroom, but it is really too peppery to eat and enjoy. However, it can be dried and ground to a powder to use like pepper.

Season July–September

Habitat Scattered in deciduous woods

Cap **Width:** 2–6″ ▪ **Shape:** Convex with a sunken, funnel-shaped center ▪ **Color:** White to cream, becoming tannish with age; flesh is white ▪ **Texture:** Smooth to slightly wrinkled

Latex White and abundant, tasting spicy-hot

Gills **Width:** Narrow ▪ **Spacing:** Crowded ▪ **Color:** White to pale cream ▪ **Attachment:** Attached

Stalk **Length:** ¾–3½″ ▪ **Width:** ½–1″ ▪ **Shape:** Straight, sometimes tapering at the end ▪ **Color:** White ▪ **Texture:** Dry with a white bloom

Spores **Spore print color:** White ▪ **Spores magnified:** Elliptical, ornamented

Look-alikes Other white *Lactarius* species

Eating raw wild mushrooms is not recommended, but if you think you might have a *Lactarius piperatus* (that is, your mushroom fits the description above), you can tear off a tiny piece of the cap, taste it, then spit it out. If it is spicy-hot, you have a Peppery Milky!

Voluminous-latex Milky

(Lactarius volemus)

David Stonner

Velvety orangish-brown cap and stalk; white gills and flesh that exude a milky white latex; has a fish-like odor

Edibility ★★★★
CHOICE. Even though the smell of this mushroom is fishy, the taste is excellent. The odor dissipates with cooking.

Season June–September

Habitat Scattered in deciduous woods

Cap **Width:** 2–5″ ▪ **Shape:** Convex, with incurved margin at first, becoming flat to vase-shaped ▪ **Color:** Orangish-brown; flesh is white, staining brown when cut ▪ **Texture:** Velvety, dry

Latex White, abundant, staining brownish, with a fish-like odor

Gills **Width:** Broad ▪ **Spacing:** Crowded ▪ **Color:** Pale cream, bruising brown ▪ **Attachment:** Attached

Stalk **Length:** 2–4″ ▪ **Width:** 3/8–3/4″ ▪ **Shape:** Equal ▪ **Color:** Orangish-brown, often the same color as the cap ▪ **Texture:** Dry

Spores **Spore print color:** White ▪ **Spores magnified:** Round, ornamented

Look-alikes The edible Hygrophorus Milky (*Lactarius hygrophoroides*, p. 51) has distant gills, no odor, and does not discolor.

The Voluminous Milky has a definite fish-like odor after handling or with age. This is a good identifying feature. The cap looks like orangish-brown velvet.

Mica Cap

(Coprinellus micaceus)

Bell-shaped, tawny brown, radially lined cap, and inky gills.

Jay Justice

Edibility ★
Edible—when young and fresh

Season April–October

Habitat In clusters around stumps or on wood debris

Cap **Width:** ½–2″ ▪ **Shape:** Egg-shaped, becoming bell-shaped ▪ **Color:** Tawny brown, darkening with age ▪ **Texture:** Covered with shiny, mica-like granules when young ▪ **Other features:** With age, cap and gills become inky and liquefy

Gills **Width:** Broad ▪ **Spacing:** Close ▪ **Color:** White, becoming dark brown, then inky black ▪ **Attachment:** Attached

Stalk **Length:** 1–3″ ▪ **Width:** ⅛–¼″ ▪ **Shape:** Thick ▪ **Color:** White, discoloring to buff ▪ **Texture:** Smooth, sometimes like felt ▪ **Other features:** Fragile, hollow

Veil *Universal veil* leaves shiny, mica-like granules on cap when young, but these disappear quickly

Spores **Spore print:** Dark brown to black ▪ **Spores magnified:** Elliptical, smooth, with small pore at tip

Look-alikes The Alcohol Inky (*Coprinopsis atramentaria*, p. 56) is fleshier and grayish.

Coprinoids or inky caps have black spores that turn wet and "inky" with age. Eventually the caps will auto-digest (dissolve into nothing). A black ink can be made by boiling the dark, liquid caps with a little water and cloves.

Also known as the Common Inky. Previously called *Coprinus micaceus.*

Alcohol Inky

(Coprinopsis atramentaria)

Jon Rapp

Gray-brown, bell-shaped, radially lined cap and inky gills

Edibility ★★ ⚠
Good, with caution. If you drink any alcoholic beverage within 1–3 days of eating this mushroom, you can become very sick, with body tingling, heart palpitations, headache and nausea. Otherwise, it is a good edible.

Season May–September

Habitat In clusters on the ground, usually near rotting or buried wood

Cap **Width:** 1½–3″ ▪ **Shape:** Egg-shaped, becoming bell-shaped ▪ **Color:** Gray to gray-brown ▪ **Texture:** Dry, smooth, silky, with minute scale remnants ▪ **Other features:** Faintly radially lined; with age, cap and gills become inky and liquefy

Gills **Width:** Broad ▪ **Spacing:** Crowded ▪ **Color:** White, becoming lavender-gray, then blackish and inky ▪ **Attachment:** Free

Stalk **Length:** 3–6″ ▪ **Width:** ¼–1″ ▪ **Shape:** Equal or slightly enlarged toward base ▪ **Color:** White ▪ **Texture:** Dry, silky, fibrous ▪ **Other features:** Hollow

Spores **Spore print color:** Black ▪ **Spores magnified:** Elliptical, smooth, with pore at tip

Look-alikes The Mica Cap (*Coprinellus micaceus*, p. 55) has a tawny-brown cap

Also called Tippler's Bane, because of the trouble it has caused for hearty drinkers. Previously called *Coprinus atramentarius.*

Shaggy Mane

(Coprinus comatus)

White, shaggy, cylindrical cap that turns black and inky

Jon Rapp

Edibility ★★★★
CHOICE. Always pick and eat this mushroom when young and fresh.

Season September–October

Habitat Often in large numbers along roadsides and in lawns and disturbed areas

Cap **Width:** 1–2½″ ▪ **Shape:** Cylindrical, 1½–6″ high, gradually expanding ▪ **Color:** White, with brownish scales ▪ **Texture:** Shaggy ▪ **Other features:** With age, cap and gills become inky and liquefy

Gills **Width:** Narrow ▪ **Spacing:** Crowded ▪ **Color:** White, becoming black and inky from the margin inward ▪ **Attachment:** Free

Stalk **Length:** 1½–8″ ▪ **Width:** ¼–¾″ ▪ **Shape:** Tall, straight, slightly bulbous at base ▪ **Color:** White ▪ **Texture:** Smooth

Spores **Spore print color:** Black ▪ **Spores magnified:** Elliptical, smooth, with small pore at tip

Look-alikes The Green-spored Lepiota (*Chlorophyllum molybdites*, p. 46) has green spores, and its cap is less cylindrical.

Though the Shaggy Mane is somewhat fragile, it can pop up in strange places—like wood chip piles, hard ground, roadsides, and even asphalt parking lots.

Scarlet Waxy Cap

(Hygrocybe coccinea)

Moist, scarlet cap with waxy, reddish-yellow gills and an orange-red stalk

Cliff White

Edibility ★
Edible

Season July–October

Habitat On the ground in mixed woods

Cap **Width:** ½–2″ ▪ **Shape:** Conical ▪ **Color:** Scarlet-blood red ▪ **Texture:** Smooth, moist

Gills **Width:** Broad ▪ **Spacing:** Close to almost distant ▪ **Color:** Bright reddish-yellow ▪ **Attachment:** Attached ▪ **Other features:** Thick, but with thin edges, waxy

Stalk **Length:** 1–3″ ▪ **Width:** ⅛–⅜″ ▪ **Shape:** Equal ▪ **Color:** Orange-red, lighter toward the base ▪ **Texture:** Moist ▪ **Other features:** Hollow

Spores **Spore print color:** White ▪ **Spores magnified:** Elliptical, smooth

Look-alikes Other *Hygrocybe* species

The Scarlet Waxy Cap is a cute mushroom—and well-named. It does look like a little red cap, and the gills really are waxy. (Rub them between your fingers, and you'll have proof.)

Fairy Ring Mushroom

(Marasmius oreades)

Tan to reddish-brown, knobbed cap, with off-white gills

Johann Bruhn

Edibility ★ ⚠

Edible—with caution (see Look-alikes).

Season May–September

Habitat In grassy areas, lawns, meadows, often in circles called fairy rings

Cap **Width:** ½–2″ ▪ **Shape:** Bell-shaped with inrolled margins, becoming convex and knobbed ▪ **Color:** Pale tan to buff to reddish-brown ▪ **Texture:** Dry, smooth, felt-like

Gills **Width:** Broad ▪ **Spacing:** Well-separated ▪ **Color:** Off-white ▪ **Attachment:** Attached or free

Stalk **Length:** 1–3″ ▪ **Width:** 1⁄16 – ¼″ ▪ **Shape:** Straight ▪ **Color:** Cream to pale buff ▪ **Texture:** Dry, tough, felt-like

Spores **Spore print color:** White ▪ **Spores magnified:** Elliptical, smooth, colorless

Look-alikes Certain poisonous *Clitocybe* and *Inocybe* species, not included in this book, can be confused with the Fairy Ring Mushroom. The poisonous Sweating Mushroom (*Clitocybe dealbata*) is gray-pink with gills running down the stalk. Poisonous *Inocybe* mushrooms usually have gray-brown gills.

Fairy rings can increase in size each year. The underground mycelium is continually spreading outward looking for nourishment, and each year when the mushrooms appear, the fairy ring is larger.

In dry weather the Fairy Ring Mushroom shrivels from lack of moisture, but after a rain these little mushrooms can magically come back to life, looking like they sprung up overnight.

Orange Pinwheel Marasmius

(Marasmius siccus)

Tiny mushroom with an orange, bell-shaped, pleated cap, white gills, and a skinny brownish stalk

Michael Kuo

Edibility ✕
Not Edible

Season July–October

Habitat Scattered to many on leaves, wood, twigs of deciduous trees

Cap **Width:** ¼–1¼″ ▪ **Shape:** Bell-shaped, becoming convex and knobbed or sunken in center ▪ **Color:** Rust-orange to orange ▪ **Texture:** With deep, wide, radial pleats

Gills **Width:** Broad ▪ **Spacing:** Distant ▪ **Color:** White to very pale yellow ▪ **Attachment:** Attached or free

Stalk **Length:** 1–2½″ ▪ **Width:** 1⁄64–1⁄32″ ▪ **Shape:** Skinny ▪ **Color:** White to pale yellow at top, shading to brownish-black at base ▪ **Texture:** Dry, tough, smooth ▪ **Other features:** Wiry and strong

Spores **Spore print color:** White ▪ **Spores magnified:** Spindle to club-shaped, smooth, large

Look-alikes Other *Marasmius* species

There are many little umbrella-like *Marasmius*, which differ mainly in color. After a good rain, they are often the first mushrooms to appear.

Recent studies suggest that *Marasmius siccus* may actually be *Marasmius fulvoferrugineus*. Stay tuned!

Bleeding Mycena

(Mycena haematopus)

Jay Justice

Small mushroom with a bell-shaped, reddish-brown cap, bleeding dark red when cut

Edibility ✕
Not Edible

Season June–September

Habitat Single to clustered on decaying wood

Cap **Width:** ½–2″ ▪ **Shape:** Egg-shaped, becoming bell-shaped to conical, with central knob and upturned margin ▪ **Color:** Reddish-pink when dry, becoming darker reddish-brown when moist, and paler gray toward the lined margins ▪ **Texture:** Dry, becoming polished and radially lined ▪ **Other features:** When cut, the flesh bleeds a dark, blood-red liquid

Gills **Width:** Narrow to moderately broad ▪ **Spacing:** Close to nearly distant ▪ **Color:** Whitish, staining a reddish-brown ▪ **Attachment:** Attached

Stalk **Length:** 1–4″ ▪ **Width:** 1⁄32–⅛″ ▪ **Shape:** Skinny ▪ **Color:** Pinkish-reddish-tan ▪ **Texture:** Covered with fine hairs; longer, coarse hairs at the base ▪ **Other features:** When cut, the stalk bleeds a dark, blood-red liquid

Spores **Spore print color:** White ▪ **Spores magnified:** Broadly elliptical, smooth, colorless

Look-alikes Other *Mycena* species—however, none "bleed" as *Mycena haematopus* does

This little mushroom is easy to identify because of the bell-shaped cap and oozing, blood-red liquid.

Orange Mycena

(Mycena leaiana)

Small, sticky, bell-shaped, orange mushroom

Jon Rapp

Edibility ✕
Not Edible

Season June–September

Habitat Dense clusters on deciduous wood

Cap **Width:** ½–2″ ▪ **Shape:** Egg-shaped, becoming bell-shaped to conical, with sunken center ▪ **Color:** Bright reddish-orange, fading to yellowish-orange ▪ **Texture:** Slimy-sticky, shiny, smooth

Gills **Width:** Broad ▪ **Spacing:** Close to crowded ▪ **Color:** Pinkish-yellow, staining orange-yellow when cut, with bright red-orange edges and a light cream inner area ▪ **Attachment:** Attached

Stalk **Length:** 1¼–2¾″ ▪ **Width:** 1/16–⅛ ▪ **Shape:** Long, equal, sometimes curving ▪ **Color:** Orange-yellow ▪ **Texture:** Tough, fibrous, sticky, with dense, long, coarse hairs at the base

Spores **Spore print color:** White ▪ **Spores magnified:** Elliptical, smooth, colorless

Look-alikes None in Missouri.

Yes, the gills of the Orange Mycena are orange—but look a little closer. You will find that only the edge of each gill is orange, and the inner portion is light cream-colored. Gills with this pattern of color are called **marginate** gills.

Pored Cap

(Boletes, a few polypores)

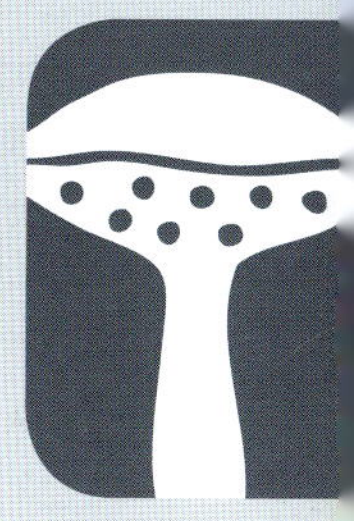

Mushrooms in this category have circular caps, central stalks, and pores on the underside of the caps. All boletes and a few polypores fit here.

Boletes—named after the taxonomic order Boletales—are rather easy to identify. They have plump, rounded caps and thick stalks, and usually grow on the ground in the woods. Most importantly, the caps have pores on the underside rather than gills. These pores are actually the openings of many tiny tubes, which form a thick, spongy layer. This tube layer separates easily from the flesh of the cap in most bolete species.

North America has lots of boletes, and there are many more bolete species in Missouri than have been described in this guide. Most are edible, but a few are considered poisonous. Better stay away from those that have orange to red pores, and also those that bruise blue.

You may have heard of porcini mushrooms, or the "King Bolete." These are popular names for *Boletus edulis*, a well-known, delicious mushroom that does not grow in Missouri. Though our state does have a lot of edible boletes, none are as tasty as the porcini. Fortunately, you can buy dried porcini in most upscale grocery stores.

A few polypores (see page 73) also fit into the "pored cap" category. They have long stalks and nearly circular caps which are pored on the underside. The caps of these polypores are tough and leathery, unlike the fleshy, spongy caps of boletes. They may appear to be growing on the ground, but are actually attached to buried roots.

Ash-tree Bolete

(Boletinellus merulioides)

Brownish, wavy cap with off-center stalk and clearly defined pores

Edibility ★
Edible

Season June–October

Habitat Scattered on the ground near ash trees

Cap **Width:** 2–5″ ▪ **Shape:** Slightly humped to flat to deeply sunken ▪ **Color:** Yellowish-brown to reddish-brown; flesh is yellowish, sometimes turning bluish-green ▪ **Texture:** Dry, dull, soft ▪ **Other features:** Margin is curved in when young; spreading, wavy and uplifted when mature

David Stonner

Pores **Size:** Large ▪ **Shape:** Shallow, uneven ▪ **Color:** Light yellowish, bruising to dark olive ▪ **Other features:** Arranged in a radial pattern, and quite beautiful

Stalk **Length:** ½–1½″ ▪ **Width:** ¼–1″ ▪ **Shape:** Thick ▪ **Color:** Brownish, bruising reddish-brown ▪ **Texture:** Dry ▪ **Other features:** Solid, off-center

Spores **Spore print color:** Olive brown ▪ **Spores magnified:** Elliptical

Look-alikes None in Missouri

The pores of the Ash Tree Bolete adhere to the cap of the mushroom. Most other boletes have easily detachable pores.

Two-colored Bolete

(Boletus bicolor)

Rose-red cap that is yellowish toward the margin; underside with tiny yellow pores; stalk reddish-yellow; all parts slowly bruising blue

Jon Rapp

Edibility ⃠
Not Recommended. Though the Two-colored Bolete is a safe and delicious edible mushroom, it is not recommended as it could be confused with other poisonous boletes that bruise blue.

Season June–October

Habitat Single to several, on the ground under oaks

Cap **Width:** 2–6″ ▪ **Shape:** Convex, becoming flat ▪ **Color:** Rose red to pinkish, yellowish toward the margin ▪ **Texture:** Dry, not shiny ▪ **Other features:** Flesh is thick, pale yellow, slowly bruising blue

Pores **Size:** Tiny ▪ **Shape:** Angular ▪ **Color:** Yellow, paler with age, slowly bruising blue

Stalk **Length:** 2–4″ ▪ **Width:** ¼–1¼″ ▪ **Shape:** Sometimes club-shaped ▪ **Color:** Pinkish-yellow with reddish tint toward the bottom ▪ **Texture:** Dry, dull, smooth ▪ **Other features:** Yellow flesh, slowly bruising blue

Spores **Spore print color:** Dull olive brown ▪ **Spores magnified:** Smooth, elliptical

Look-alikes Other *Boletus* species, some of which may be poisonous. Avoid boletes with orange to red pores, and those that bruise blue.

The beautiful red cap and the contrasting bright yellow of the underside are what give the Two-colored Bolete its name. "Bruising blue is not for you."

Frost's Bolete

(Boletus frostii)

Blood red cap with red pores and a red, webbed stalk; all parts bruising blue

David Stonner

Edibility ⃠
Not Recommended. Though the Frost's Bolete is actually an edible mushroom, it is not recommended because it could be confused with other poisonous red-pored boletes.

Season June–October

Habitat Scattered on the ground in oak woods

Cap **Width:** 2–6″ ▪ **Shape:** Convex becoming flat ▪ **Color:** Blood red ▪ **Texture:** Sticky, slimy ▪ **Other features:** Flesh is yellowish, instantly bruising blue

Pores **Size:** Small ▪ **Shape:** Round ▪ **Color:** Deep red, bruising blue

Stalk **Length:** 1½–4¾″ ▪ **Width:** ½–1″ ▪ **Shape:** Usually straight, sometimes curving at the base ▪ **Color:** Blood red, with yellowish raised webbing; bruises blue ▪ **Texture:** Webbed

Spores **Spore print color:** Olive brown ▪ **Spores magnified:** Smooth, elliptical

Look-alikes Other *Boletus* species, some of which may be poisonous. Avoid boletes with orange to red pores, and those that bruise blue.

"Pores of red—may put you to bed!"

Pallid Bolete

(Boletus pallidus)

Pale cream-buff cap and stalk with pale cream-yellow pores

Michael Kuo

Edibility ★
Edible

Season June–September

Habitat Single to several, on the ground in oak woods

Cap **Width:** 1½–6″ ▪ **Shape:** Convex becoming flat ▪ **Color:** Pale cream-buff ▪ **Texture:** Dull, dry, suede-like

Pores **Size:** Small ▪ **Shape:** Circular, becoming angular ▪ **Color:** Pale cream-yellow, sometimes weakly bruising blue, then brownish

Stalk **Length:** 2–4¾″ ▪ **Width:** ½–1¼″ ▪ **Shape:** Enlarging slightly toward the base ▪ **Color:** Pale cream-buff, might be reddish at the base ▪ **Texture:** Smooth

Spores **Spore print color:** Olive brown ▪ **Spores magnified:** Barely spindle-shaped

Look-alikes Other *Boletus* species

The definition of the word *pallid* is "pale or deficient in color." The Pallid Bolete certainly fits that description, as it is mostly pale cream-buff to very pale yellow.

Black-footed Polypore

(Polyporus badius)

Smooth, wavy brown cap with whitish-tannish pores on the underside and a black, smooth, off-center stalk

Michael Kuo

Edibility ✕
Not Edible

Season August–October, but can overwinter

Habitat Single to several on dead wood and stumps of deciduous trees

Cap **Width:** 2–8″ ▪ **Shape:** Convex to funnel-shaped ▪ **Color:** Dark reddish-brownish, becoming darker with age ▪ **Texture:** Dry, smooth, tough, leathery

Pores **Size:** Tiny ▪ **Shape:** Circular, sometimes with angles ▪ **Color:** Whitish-tannish

Stalk **Length:** ½–2½″ ▪ **Width:** ⅛–⅝″ ▪ **Shape:** Equal ▪ **Color:** Blackish ▪ **Texture:** Smooth ▪ **Other features:** Off-center, tough

Spores **Spore print color:** White ▪ **Spores magnified:** Cylindrical, elliptical, smooth, colorless

Look-alikes The Rooting Polypore (*Polyporus radicatus*, p. 69) is fleshier and the stalk continues underground with a root-like filament.

When you see the black, off-center stalk of the Black-footed Polypore, you'll easily figure out what it is.

Rooting Polypore

(Polyporus radicatus)

Johann Bruhn

Scruffy, tough, yellowish-brown cap with whitish-yellow pores; stalk with a long, black, root-like filament

Edibility ✕
Not Edible

Season August–October

Habitat Usually single, on the ground near stumps or attached to buried roots

Cap **Width:** 1½–10″ ▪ **Shape:** Convex to sunken ▪ **Color:** Yellowish-brown ▪ **Texture:** Tough, dry, scruffy

Pores **Size:** Tiny ▪ **Shape:** Angular ▪ **Color:** Whitish-yellowish

Stalk **Length:** 2½–6″ ▪ **Width:** ¼–1″ ▪ **Shape:** Equal, or enlarged toward the base ▪ **Color:** Dingy yellow ▪ **Texture:** Scruffy to scaly ▪ **Other features:** Central, with a long, black, root-like, underground filament

Spores **Spore print color:** White ▪ **Spores magnified:** Elliptical, smooth, colorless

Look-alikes The Black-footed Polypore (*Polyporus badius*, p. 68) is thin and leathery, and its stalk does not have a root-like filament.

This is the only fall Missouri polypore with a stalk that has a long, black, root-like underground filament.

Old Man of the Woods

(Strobilomyces floccopus) and Confusing Old Man of the Woods *(S. confusus)*

Grayish-black, shaggy cap with grayish pores, and a grayish-black, shaggy stalk

Cliff White

Edibility ★
Edible, when young and fresh. As it ages, the "Old Man" becomes crusty, wimpy and tasteless.

Season July–October

Habitat Usually single, on the ground in mixed hardwoods

Cap **Width:** 2–6″ ▪ **Shape:** Cushion-shaped, becoming flat ▪ **Color:** Grayish-black; white flesh showing between dark scales ▪ **Texture:** *S. floccopus* is covered with large, shaggy, soft, flattened scales; *S. confusus* has erect, firm warts ▪ **Other features:** Flesh is whitish, bruising coral-red, then black

Pores **Size:** Small ▪ **Shape:** Angular ▪ **Color:** Grayish, bruising reddish then black

Stalk **Length:** 2–5″ ▪ **Width:** ½–1″ ▪ **Shape:** Slightly enlarged toward the base ▪ **Color:** Grayish-black ▪ **Texture:** Wooly, shaggy ▪ **Other features:** Solid, with two wooly rings

Veil *Partial veil* grayish, leaving a couple of wooly rings on the stalk

Spores **Spore print color:** Black ▪ **Spores magnified:** Elliptical

Look-alikes The Onusta Amanita (*Amanita onusta*, p. 42) has gills, not pores. For many years, mushroom field guides have stated that the Old Man of the Woods has shaggy, flattened scales on the cap, while the Confusing Old Man of the Woods has erect, firm warts or spines on the cap. However, recent studies of their spores have shown little difference between these two mushrooms.

Although both the Old Man and the Confusing Old Man are edible, neither has a lot of appeal. These two mushrooms are common, unusual, and kind of cute in an odd way.

Bitter Bolete

(Tylopilus felleus)

Large, tannish-brown cap with pinkish-white pores, and a webbed, tannish-brown stalk

Edibility ✕
Not Edible

Season June–November

Habitat Single or scattered, on the ground in mixed woods

Cap **Width:** 2–6″ ▪ **Shape:** Convex, becoming flat ▪ **Color:** Tannish-brown to buff ▪ **Texture:** Sticky when wet ▪ **Other features:** Flesh is thick, white

Pores **Size:** Small ▪ **Shape:** Round ▪ **Color:** Pinkish-white, turning pale pink with age

Stalk **Length:** 1½–4″ ▪ **Width:** ¼–1¼″ ▪ **Shape:** Thick, enlarging toward the base ▪ **Color:** Tannish-brown, sometimes bruising brownish, with brown webbing ▪ **Texture:** With webbing, sometimes raised

Spores **Spore print color:** Burgundy brown ▪ **Spores magnified:** Smooth, elliptical

Look-alikes Other boletes, some of which may be edible—especially the choice King Bolete (*Boletus edulis*), which does not grow in Missouri.

If you are tempted to taste, beware! The Bitter Bolete is *very* bitter.

Violet-gray Bolete

(Tylopilus plumbeoviolaceus)

Large, violet-gray cap with cream-pink pores; violet stalk, sometimes webbed

cc by Dan Molter

Edibility ✕
Not Edible. The Violet-gray Bolete is quite bitter.

Season June–September

Habitat Scattered on the ground in mixed woods

Cap **Width:** 1½–7″ ▪ **Shape:** Convex, becoming flat ▪ **Color:** Violet, turning grayish-purple, then brownish ▪ **Texture:** Dry, smooth ▪ **Other features:** Flesh is white

Pores **Size:** Small ▪ **Shape:** Round ▪ **Color:** Cream becoming pinkish-tan

Stalk **Length:** 3–4½″ ▪ **Width:** ¼–1¼″ ▪ **Shape:** Enlarging slightly toward the base ▪ **Color:** Violet, even after cap fades; sometimes becoming webbed with a darker violet ▪ **Texture:** Smooth

Spores **Spore print color:** Pinkish-reddish-brown ▪ **Spores magnified:** Smooth, elliptical

Look-alikes Other *Boletus* species

Although it turns brownish with age, in its prime the Violet-gray Bolete is a beautiful mushroom.

Pored Bracket

(Most polypores)

The typical "pored bracket" has a roughly semicircular cap that is attached to wood, either directly or by a very short, off-center stalk. It may look like a fan, shelf or hoof. Check the underside of the cap and you will find pores, not gills. Pored-bracket fungi are commonly called polypores, after the taxonomic order Polyporales.

These very common fungi are the ones you see sticking out like shelves from the trunks of living and dead trees, or growing in overlapping layers on logs and fallen branches. Generally they are too leathery or woody to eat, but a few are tender and edible at the growing edges, or when young.

I've divided the pored brackets into two subcategories—single and layered—for easier identification.

Single—Brackets that grow singly or with a few others; may be hoof-like and woody

Layered—Brackets that grow in layered groups; often fan-shaped and leathery

Be aware, however, that these subcategories blend into each other. "Single" polypores sometimes may be found in groups, and "layered" polypores may occasionally appear singly. Think of single and layered as general guidelines that Mother Nature usually follows, but not always!

Thin-maze Flat Polypore

(Daedaleopsis confragosa)

Grayish-brown cap, top is zoned and has a furrowed underside resembling a maze

Edibility ✕
Not Edible

Season June–December, but can be found all year

Habitat Single or in small layered clusters on dead wood or in wounds of living trees, in deciduous woods

Cap **Width:** 1–6″ ▪ **Shape:** Shelf-like ▪ **Color:** Concentric zones of gray to brown ▪ **Texture:** Corky, firm

Pores **Shape:** Circular or elongated, maze-like ▪ **Color:** White to brownish, sometimes bruising pink

Stalk Not present

Spores **Spore print color:** White ▪ **Spores magnified:** Cylindrical, smooth, curved, colorless

Look-alikes The Hexagonal-pored Polypore (*Polyporus alveolaris*, p. 79) has hexagonal pores.

The pattern on the underside of the Thin-maze Flat Polypore is quite beautiful! Take a look with a lens. Also known as *Daedalea confragosa.*

Beefsteak Polypore

(Fistulina hepatica)

Thick, semi-circular, red-rust, gelatinous cap and pinkish-yellow underside

Jon Rapp

Edibility ★★

Good, when young and fresh. The taste is acidic and sour, and the texture is squishy and liver-like. That being said, the Beefsteak Polypore is delicious after marinating overnight and adding to lentils or a grain (or both).

Season July–October

Habitat Single to several at the base of living oaks, and on stumps

Cap **Width:** 3–20″ ▪ **Shape:** Semi-circular or spoon-shaped ▪ **Color:** Red-rust ▪ **Texture:** Gelatinous, smooth ▪ **Other features:** Flesh is thick, dark pinkish, mottled with lighter veining

Pores **Shape:** Circular ▪ **Color:** Whitish, becoming reddish-brown

Stalk (if present) **Length:** Very short ▪ **Width:** Thick ▪ **Shape:** Broad, then tapered ▪ **Color:** Blood-red

Spores **Spore print color:** Pinkish-salmon ▪ **Spores magnified:** Smooth, oval

Look-alikes None in Missouri

Fistulina means "small pipes," referring to the tubes on the underside of the Beefsteak Polypore. The tubes are very small and closely packed but do not touch each other. *Hepatica* means "liver," and this mushroom really does look like a liver from a large animal. It also has a strong resemblance to a thick piece of beef.

Artist Conk

(Ganoderma applanatum)

Woody, semi-circular, brownish cap with a white underside that bruises dark gray to black

Jon Rapp

Edibility ✕
Not Edible

Season Year-round

Habitat Single to several on dead wood or in wounds of living deciduous trees

Cap **Width:** 2–20″ ▪ **Shape:** Shelf-like, semi-circular ▪ **Color:** Brown to grayish black ▪ **Texture:** Woody, can be warty or zoned; very hard, not shiny

Pores **Shape:** Circular ▪ **Color:** White when fresh, bruising dark gray to black ▪ **Other features:** Pore surface darkens when scratched

Stalk Not present

Spores **Spore print color:** Brown ▪ **Spores magnified:** Elliptical, blunt at one end

Look-alikes Other *Ganoderma* species, but the Artist Conk is pure white on the underside when fresh. The Resinous Polypore (*Ischnoderma resinosum*, p. 78) exudes amber-colored droplets of moisture when young.

There are many shelf mushrooms, and some have a white underside that darkens when scratched, but the Artist Conk is the largest and the best for drawing and writing.

These mushrooms have been used for art and communication throughout history. When you find one, make sure you draw a picture on the underside with a pointed instrument. Let it dry and your creation will be a permanent piece of art.

Ling Chih

(Ganoderma lucidum)

Hard, usually flat, zoned cap, with reddish-brown, shiny top

Edibility ★ ℞

Edible/Medicinal. The Ling Chih is too tough to be a good edible, but in China it is used medicinally to promote longevity and good health. It is also thought to prevent cancer. Recent studies in the West have shown that the Ling Chih stimulates the body's immune system. It can be ground or purchased commercially and steeped for tea. The flavor of the tea is strong and bitter, but can be balanced with honey or sugar.

Season May–November

Habitat Single to several, at the base of living and dead deciduous trees; could also be around stumps

Cap **Width:** 1–14″ ▪ **Shape:** Shelf-like, semi-circular ▪ **Color:** Dark red to dark brown, lighter toward margin ▪ **Texture:** Hard, shiny, often zoned

Pores **Shape:** Circular to angular ▪ **Color:** Whitish to brown

Stalk Rarely present

Spores **Spore print color:** Brown ▪ **Spores magnified:** Elliptical, with double wall

Look-alikes Other *Ganoderma* species. The Resinous Polypore (*Ischnoderma resinosum*, p. 78) exudes amber-colored droplets of moisture when young.

Ling Chih means "mushroom of immortality." Also known as the Reishi mushroom.

Resinous Polypore

(Ischnoderma resinosum)

Large, thick, hairy, brownish cap with thick margin and whitish pores

Michael Kuo

Resin

Jon Rapp

Edibility ★★
Good, when young and fresh. Take only the soft, fleshy outer edges, and sauté. They are surprisingly good.

Season September–October

Habitat Single to several on logs and stumps of deciduous trees

Cap **Width:** 3–10″ ▪ **Shape:** Semi-circular with thick, rounded margin ▪ **Color:** Ochre to dark brown, becoming blackish and concentrically zoned ▪ **Texture:** Finely hairy, fleshy when young, sometimes exuding a resinous, watery liquid; later becoming firm and hard with a black resinous crust

Pores **Shape:** Circular to angular ▪ **Color:** Whitish to light brownish, bruising darker

Stalk Not present

Spores **Spore print color:** White ▪ **Spores magnified:** Cylindrical, smooth

Look-alikes *Ganoderma* species are woody and hard at all stages and have a brownish-red, varnished-looking crust.

When very young, the Resinous Polypore will often ooze amber-colored droplets of moisture.

Hexagonal-pored Polypore

(Polyporus alveolaris)

Cliff White

Reddish-yellow, fan-shaped cap, scaly on top; underside with rows of white, six-sided, radially arranged pores

Edibility ★
Edible. Though this is considered an edible mushroom, it is tough and woody. I wouldn't recommend taking your time to pick and eat it.

Season May–November

Habitat Single or in groups on dead branches of deciduous trees

Cap **Width:** 3⁄8–4″ ▪ **Shape:** Semicircular, fan-shaped ▪ **Color:** Reddish-yellow to pale red, with concentric bands of color ▪ **Texture:** Scaly, becoming smooth

Pores **Shape:** Six-sided, honeycombed, usually in radial rows ▪ **Color:** White, drying yellow

Stalk (if present) **Length:** Short ▪ **Width:** Thick ▪ **Shape:** Stubby ▪ **Color:** White, drying yellow

Spores **Spore print color:** White ▪ **Spores magnified:** Cylindrical, smooth, colorless

Look-alikes The pores of the Thin-maze Flat Polypore (*Daedaleopsis confragosa*, p. 74) have a more maze-like arrangement.

The underside of the Hexagonal-pored Polypore is amazingly beautiful. Make sure to look at it through a lens. Previously called *Favolus alveolaris.*

Cinnabar Polypore

(Pycnoporus cinnabarinus)

Tough, fan-shaped, bright red-orange cap and underside

Cliff White

Edibility ✕
Not Edible

Season Year-round

Habitat Single to several on dead deciduous branches, twigs and wood, mainly oak

Cap **Width:** 1–5″ ▪ **Shape:** Semi-circular, flat ▪ **Color:** Bright cinnabar-red to orange-red ▪ **Texture:** Finely hairy

Pores **Shape:** Angular, irregular ▪ **Color:** Bright cinnabar-red to orange-red, same color as the cap

Stalk Not present

Spores **Spore print color:** White ▪ **Spores magnified:** Cylindrical, curved, smooth

Look-alikes No other small Missouri polypore is bright red-orange on the cap and on the underside.

The Cinnabar Polypore is easy to spot, as both the top and underside are the same color—bright cinnabar-red to orange-red.

Chicken of the Woods

(Laetiporus cincinnatus)

Layered, fan-shaped, fleshy caps that are orange to pale orange on top and white on the underside

Jon Rapp

Edibility ★★★★
CHOICE. Some people think the pale Chicken of the Woods (*Laetiporus cincinnatus*) is more tender than the sulfur-colored Chicken of the Woods (*Laetiporus sulphureus*, p. 82). (For recipes, see pages 151–153.)

Season May–November

Habitat In overlapping clusters on stumps, trunks and logs of dead or dying deciduous trees. Can also be on living trees and buried roots.

Each Cap **Width:** 2–12″ ▪ **Shape:** Flat, fan-shaped or semicircular ▪ **Color:** Light orange when fresh, turning pale orange with age ▪ **Texture:** Fleshy

Pores **Shape:** Angular ▪ **Color:** White or off-white

Stalk Not present

Spores **Spore print color:** White ▪ **Spores magnified:** Elliptical to round

Look-alikes The sulfur-colored Chicken of the Woods (*Laetiporus sulphureus*, p. 82) has a sulfur-yellow underside. No other Missouri mushrooms have the color, shape and growing habit of the two "chicks" (*Laetiporus cincinnatus* and *L. sulphureus*).

It's easy to tell the two species of "chicks" apart. The underside of *Laetiporus cincinnatus* is white, and the underside of *L. sulphureus* (p. 82) is bright yellow. *Laetiporus cincinnatus* is sometimes called Chicken Mushroom.

Chicken of the Woods

or Sulfur Shelf
(Laetiporus sulphureus)

Maxine Stone

Layered, fan-shaped, fleshy caps that are orange-red to orange-yellow on top and sulfur-yellow on the underside

Edibility ★★★★
CHOICE. Chicken and biscuits, anyone? (For recipes, see pages 151–153.) Although this is a safe and delicious mushroom, some people get a bit of stomach upset or swollen lips after eating it. Try just a small amount the first time.

Season May–November

Habitat In overlapping clusters on stumps, trunks and logs of dead or dying deciduous trees. Can also be on living trees and buried roots.

Each Cap **Width:** 2–12″ ▪ **Shape:** Flat, fan-shaped or semicircular ▪ **Color:** Orange-red to orange-yellow when fresh, turning lighter with age ▪ **Texture:** Fleshy

Pores **Shape:** Angular ▪ **Color:** Bright sulfur-yellow

Stalk Not present

Spores **Spore print color:** White ▪ **Spores magnified:** Elliptical to round

Look-alikes The pale Chicken of the Woods (*Laetiporus cincinnatus*, p. 81) is white on the underside. No other Missouri mushrooms have the color, shape and growing habit of the two "chicks" (*Laetiporus sulphureus* and *L. cincinnatus*).

The two "chicks" can grow very large, with up to 50 overlapping caps in a cluster. They are both called Chicken of the Woods because they have the texture of chicken, and with a little imagination can taste like chicken. *Laetiporus sulphureus* is also called Chicken Mushroom.

Dryad's Saddle

(Polyporus squamosus)

Jon Rapp

Large, fleshy, scaly, yellowish-tan cap with large, yellowish-white pores and a short stalk; smells like watermelon rind

Edibility ★★
Good. If you find the Dryad's Saddle you can cut off the tender edges and cook them up. They are reasonably good—especially when the mushroom is young.

Season May–October

Habitat Single or layered, on living or dead deciduous wood

Cap **Width:** 2½–12″ ▪ **Shape:** Circular to fan-shaped ▪ **Color:** Yellowish-tan ▪ **Texture:** Covered with dark hairy scales

Pores **Shape:** Large, angular ▪ **Color:** Yellowish-white

Stalk **Length:** ½–2″ ▪ **Width:** ½–1½″ ▪ **Shape:** Stub-like ▪ **Color:** Blackish at base ▪ **Other features:** Off-center, tough

Spores **Spore print color:** White ▪ **Spores magnified:** Oblong, elliptical, smooth

Look-alikes Other polypores, none of which are known to be poisonous

The Dryad's Saddle smells like watermelon rind.

Try this little recipe: Cut the tender parts into smaller pieces and cook in butter. Drain and pat dry. Make a sugar syrup and pour evenly over all. Refrigerate. Believe it or not, this tastes like watermelon candy.

False Turkey Tail

(Stereum ostrea)

Large groups of leathery, parchment-like caps with multi-colored zones and a smooth underside

David Stonner

Edibility ✕
Not Edible

Season Year-round

Habitat In large, layered groups on stumps and logs of deciduous trees. They like oaks.

Cap **Width:** ½ –4″ ▪ **Shape:** Semi-circular, irregular ▪ **Color:** Zones of browns, rusts, greens ▪ **Texture:** Leathery, hairy

Underside Buff-colored, smooth

Stalk Not present

Spores **Spore print color:** White ▪ **Spores magnified:** Cylindrical, smooth

Look-alikes The Turkey Tail (*Trametes versicolor*, p. 85) has pores on the underside. The Multi-color Gill Polypore (*Lenzites betulina*, p. 88) has a gill-like underside.

Michael Kuo

The False Turkey Tail is very, very, very common. Although it has a smooth (not pored) underside, it looks and grows like a pored bracket—so I have placed it in this category. *Ostrea* is the Latin word for "oyster."

Turkey Tail

(Trametes versicolor)

Layered clusters of leathery, thin caps with multi-colored zones and whitish-yellow pores

David Stonner

Jon Rapp

Edibility ★ ℞
Edible/Medicinal. The Chinese use the Turkey Tail as a remedy against liver cancer and jaundice. It can be ground and used as a tea or in soup.

Season Year-round

Habitat In groups, rows or clusters, often layered, on stumps and logs of deciduous trees.

Cap **Width:** 1–4″ ▪ **Shape:** Semi-circular to spoon-shaped, irregular, thin ▪ **Color:** Zones of black-green, gray-blue, gray-brown, ochre-rust ▪ **Texture:** Leathery, with alternately hairy and smooth zones

Pores **Shape:** Angular ▪ **Color:** Whitish-yellow

Stalk Not present

Spores **Spore print color:** White ▪ **Spores magnified:** Cylindrical, smooth

Look-alikes The False Turkey Tail (*Stereum ostrea*, p. 84) is parchment-like and has a smooth underside. The Multi-color Gill Polypore (*Lenzites betulina*, p. 88) has a gill-like underside.

The bands of colors on the cap make the Turkey Tail easy to recognize. The margin is always lightest in color. It is very common.

Violet Toothed Polypore

(Trichaptum biforme)

David Stonner

Tough, hairy caps with violet margins and zones of white, brown and black; underside with whitish-violet pores that break into teeth

Edibility ✕
Not Edible

Season Year-round

Habitat Single or in layered groups on stumps and logs of deciduous wood

Cap **Width:** ¼–3″ ▪ **Shape:** Semi-circular, flat ▪ **Color:** Zones of white-gray, ochre-dark brown, brown-black; persistent violet along the margin ▪ **Texture:** Tough, hairy

Pores **Shape:** Angular, becoming tooth-like ▪ **Color:** Whitish-brown with violet tinge and fading to buff, persistent violet along margin

Stalk Not present

Spores **Spore print color:** White ▪ **Spores magnified:** Cylindrical, smooth

Look-alikes Other flat polypores that grow on stumps and logs

The Violet Toothed Polypore is very common. You might see hundreds of them happily eating away at tree stumps and logs. *Biforme* means "having two forms." This is a reference to the underside of the mushroom, which can be pored or tooth-like.

Gilled Bracket

(A few polypores, *Pleurotus*)

This is what you might call an "oddball" category. It contains four bracket-shaped fungi that grow on wood, but have gills or gill-like structures on the underside instead of pores. The first two species in this category are polypores, the third is a fleshy and delicious agaric (the Oyster, *Pleurotus ostreatus* or *P. pulmonarius*, p. 90), and mycologists are still debating about the fourth (the Common Split Gill, *Schizophyllum commune*, p. 91). It could be a polypore, an agaric, or who knows!

Although there are only a few of these oddballs, they can be confusing to a beginner, so I have placed them in a group of their own.

(If you are wondering what a "gill-like structure" is, take a look at the photo of the Common Split Gill on page 91. A picture is worth a thousand words!)

Multi-color Gill Polypore

(Lenzites betulina)

Semi-circular, tough, hairy, multicolored, zoned cap; underside white, with leathery gill-like tubes

Edibility ✕
Not Edible

Season July–November

Habitat Single or in layered groups on dead deciduous wood

Cap **Width:** 1–4″ ▪ **Shape:** Semi-circular ▪ **Color:** Concentric orange and brown zones, although sometimes white, cream, grayish or brownish ▪ **Texture:** Tough, hairy ▪ **Other features:** Often greenish because of algae growing in the hairs

Underside White, with leathery gill-like tubes which are radially arranged, forked and fused

Stalk Not present

Spores **Spore print color:** White ▪ **Spores magnified:** Cylindrical, smooth, colorless

Look-alikes The Turkey Tail (*Trametes versicolor*, p. 85) doesn't have a gill-like underside. The False Turkey Tail (*Stereum ostrea*, p. 84) has a smooth underside.

The "gills" of the Multi-color Gill Polypore are actually radially arranged tubes that are forked and fused, which can make them look like gills. These tubes are tough and leathery, as opposed to true gills, which are more fragile.

Also called Birch Polypore, though it will be found on many trees in addition to birches.

Coral-pink Merulius

(Phlebia incarnata)

Small, semi-circular, pinkish-coral cap with a pinkish-cream, wrinkled and veined underside

Patrick Harvey

Edibility ✕
Not Edible

Season September–October

Habitat Single or layered on dead logs and stumps of deciduous trees

Cap **Width:** ¾–1½″ ▪ **Shape:** Semi-circular with wavy margin ▪ **Color:** Pinkish-coral, turning salmon-cream ▪ **Texture:** Finely hairy

Underside Pinkish to cream, pore-like with radiating, wrinkled and veined, branched folds

Stalk Not present

Spores **Spore print color:** White ▪ **Spores magnified:** Elliptical, smooth, colorless

Look-alikes None in Missouri

The color of the cap of this mushroom is unusual and pleasing. Previously called *Merulius incarnatus.*

Oyster Mushroom

(Pleurotus ostreatus and *P. pulmonarius)*

Broad, fleshy, whitish-grayish-tan cap, with a stub-like, off-center stalk

Jon Rapp

Edibility ★★★★
CHOICE. (For recipe, see page 162.)

Season *Pleurotus ostreatus* fruits year-round, especially after a good rain and when the weather is mild. *P. pulmonarius* fruits only during warm months.

Habitat In clusters on stumps, logs and trunks of deciduous trees

Cap **Width:** *P. ostreatus* 1–6"; *P. pulmonarius* is smaller ▪ **Shape:** Shell-shaped, semi-circular to elongated; margin is lobed to wavy ▪ **Color:** Whitish to grayish to tan ▪ **Texture:** Velvety ▪ **Other features:** Flesh is thick, white

Gills **Width:** narrow to broad ▪ **Spacing:** Close to nearly distant ▪ **Color:** White becoming yellowish ▪ **Attachment:** Descending the stalk

Stalk (If present) **Length:** ¼–1¼" ▪ **Width:** ¼–¾" ▪ **Shape:** Short, thick ▪ **Color:** White ▪ **Texture:** Base is hairy ▪ **Other features:** Off-center, solid

Spores **Spore print color:** White to grayish-lilac ▪ **Spores magnified:** Narrowly elliptical, smooth, colorless

Look-alikes None in Missouri that are poisonous

The flavor of the wild Oyster Mushroom is far superior to the store-bought variety. Then again, all freshly picked wild mushrooms are better that store-bought—whether locally cultivated or freshly imported.

Common Split Gill

(Schizophyllum commune)

Clusters of small, white, hairy, fan-shaped caps; undersides with whitish or pinkish gill-like folds, splitting toward edge

David Stonner

Edibility ✕
Not Edible

Season Year-round

Habitat In groups on dead branches of deciduous trees

Cap **Width:** ¼–1½″ ▪ **Shape:** Fan-shaped ▪ **Color:** Whitish-grayish ▪ **Texture:** Dry, hairy, leathery

Underside Whitish-grayish-pinkish, hairy, with gill-like folds that are split lengthwise to the cap margin

Stalk Not present, or tiny

Spores **Spore print color:** White ▪ **Spores magnified:** Cylindrical, smooth

Look-alikes None in Missouri

This is a very common and cute little mushroom. It's easy to identify if you check for the split gills underneath the cap.

Rosette

(A few polypores, *Sparassis*)

When you find one of these mushrooms, I bet you'll know it! They tend to be large, sometimes even huge, and have a distinctive look. The general shape is round and multi-layered: think of a big, brown, fluffed-up chicken, or a giant cream-colored rose, or a huge yellowish cauliflower. The layers within the rosette seem to radiate from, or revolve around, one or more central points.

These four rosette mushrooms are all good edibles. Look for them on the ground, near the bases of living or decaying trees, often oaks.

Berkeley's Polypore

(Bondarzewia berkeleyi)

One to many fleshy, cream-colored caps, in a layered cluster or rosette, with whitish pores that descend the stalk

Patrick Harvey

Edibility ★★★
Excellent. When young and easy to cut, the Berkeley's Polypore can be eaten and is quite good. Cut the softer, outer edges of the caps (also called "leaves"). This mushroom gets tough, woody and bitter with age.

Season July–October

Habitat One or more large clusters, on the ground near the bases of deciduous trees, especially oaks. (See photo on page 7.)

Fruiting Body **Width:** Up to 3 ft.

Each Cap **Width:** 3–12″ ▪ **Shape:** Wide, convex or flat, becoming depressed in the center ▪ **Color:** Cream ▪ **Texture:** Dry, hairy or smooth, can be rough or pitted ▪ **Other features:** Flesh white, thick, firm, becoming tough; odor mild and earthy, becoming strong

Pores **Shape:** Wide, angular, often torn ▪ **Color:** Whitish, becoming dingy ▪ **Other features:** Descending stalk

Stalk **Length:** 2–4″ ▪ **Width:** 1–2″ ▪ **Shape:** Rooting ▪ **Color:** Yellowish

Spores **Spore print color:** White ▪ **Spores magnified:** Round, colorless, warted

Look-alikes The Hen of the Woods (*Grifola frondosa*, p. 95) has many smaller, grayish to brownish caps. The Black-staining Polypore (*Meripilus sumstinei*, p. 96) blackens when bruised or handled. The Eastern Cauliflower Mushroom (*Sparassis spatulata*, p. 97) has ribbon-like folds.

This mushroom can be very large—up to three feet wide and weighing 50 pounds or more.

Hen of the Woods

(Grifola frondosa)

Large circular cluster of spoon-shaped caps, each grayish-brown on top and white beneath, emerging from a branching whitish base

Edibility ★★★★ ℞
CHOICE/Medicinal. Not only is this a deliciously choice mushroom, but it also is known to have many health benefits, including support for the immune system and improvements in blood pressure, blood sugar and cholesterol levels. Hen of the Woods also makes a hearty and meaty mushroom soup. Mmmm! (For recipes, see pages 156, 157 and 163.)

Season September–November

Habitat A single large circular cluster, on the ground at the base of oak trees.

Fruiting Body **Width:** Up to 3 ft.

Each Cap **Width:** ¾–3″ ▪ **Shape:** Spoon- or fan-shaped ▪ **Color:** Grayish to grayish-brownish to brownish

Pores **Shape:** Angular ▪ **Color:** White to yellowish

Stalk **Length:** Short ▪ **Shape:** Branching ▪ **Color:** White

Spores **Spore print color:** White ▪ **Spores magnified:** Elliptical, smooth

Look-alikes The Black-staining Polypore (*Meripilus sumstinei*, p. 96) blackens when bruised or handled. Berkeley's Polypore (*Bondarzewia berkeleyi*, p. 94) is thick-fleshed and cream-colored. The Eastern Cauliflower Mushroom (*Sparassis spatulata*, p. 97) has ribbon-like folds.

The Hen of the Woods is often found in the same area year after year, so check your spot every autumn. Individual clusters can weigh up to 100 pounds. The Hen of the Woods is also called Maitake.

Black-staining Polypore

(Meripilus sumstinei)

Michael Kuo

Many fleshy, grayish-yellow, fan-shaped caps in large circular clusters; caps bruise black when cut or touched

Edibility ★★

Good—when young and fresh. The Black-staining Polypore has a lovely, earthy odor. Though this mushroom is not terribly appealing as it blackens, when young and easy to cut it can be eaten and is quite good. Use only the softer, outer edges of the caps.

Season July–September

Habitat In large circular clusters, on the ground around stumps of living deciduous trees, especially oaks.

Fruiting Body **Width:** Up to 32″

Each Cap **Width:** 2–8″ ▪ **Shape:** Fan-shaped, semi-circular or spoon-shaped, with a thin, sharp margin ▪ **Color:** Grayish to dull yellowish, darkening along margin; bruises black when cut or touched ▪ **Texture:** Fleshy

Pores **Shape:** Angular, often torn ▪ **Color:** White, bruising black

Stalk (If present) **Length:** Very short ▪ **Width:** Thick ▪ **Texture:** Fibrous

Spores **Spore print color:** White ▪ **Spores magnified:** Elliptical to round, smooth, colorless

Look-alikes Berkeley's polypore (*Bondarzewia berkeleyi*, p. 94) is thick-fleshed and cream-colored. Hen of the Woods (*Grifola frondosa*, p. 95) has many smaller, grayish-brownish caps. The Eastern Cauliflower Mushroom (*Sparassis spatulata*, p. 97) has ribbon-like folds. None of these look-alikes bruise black.

The Black-staining Polypore can be found in very large clusters measuring up to 32" across. Previously called *Meripilus giganteus.*

Eastern Cauliflower Mushroom

(Sparassis spatulata)

Maxine Stone

Large, stalkless, whitish-yellow rosette with flattened, wavy, ribbon-like folds

Edibility ★★★
Excellent—when young and fresh. If you should find this mushroom you're in luck. You could possibly have several meals off of it! (For recipe, see page 169.)

Season July–October

Habitat Single, often at the base of decayed oak stumps

Fruiting Body **Width:** 6–12″ ▪ **Height:** 6–10″ ▪ **Shape:** Large rosette with flattened, wavy, ribbon-like folds ▪ **Color:** Whitish-yellow ▪ **Texture:** Smooth ▪ **Other features:** With a cord-like root at the base; flesh is flexible when young, becoming tough with age

Spores **Spore print color:** White ▪ **Spores magnified:** Oval, smooth, colorless

Look-alikes The Hen of the Woods (*Grifola frondosa*, p. 95) has many small, grayish to brownish caps. The Black-staining Polypore (*Meripilus sumstinei*, p. 96) blackens when bruised or handled. Berkeley's Polypore (*Bondarzewia berkeleyi*, p. 94) is thick-fleshed and cream-colored.

The Eastern Cauliflower Mushroom can be quite common when we have a good, wet summer. However, it is rare in a dry summer. It is unusual-looking and easy to identify. Think of a wavy whitish-yellow ribbon.

Also known as *Sparassis herbstii,* and often confused with *Sparassis crispa,* which is rare and CHOICE. *Sparassis* is derived from the Greek "I tear to pieces."

Vase

(Chanterelles, *Hypomyces*)

This category of vase- or trumpet-shaped mushrooms includes the famous edible group known as the chanterelles, and the strange and delicious Lobster (*Hypomyces lactifluorum*, p. 104). "Vase" mushrooms come in distinctive colors—orange, yellowish orange, reddish orange, and black—and grow on the ground.

The vase shape can be a bit tricky to identify, for two reasons. First, these mushrooms may not appear vase-like when very young, and often become flattened as they age. For identification purposes, look for specimens that are neither very young nor over-mature.

Secondly, many different agarics (including species of *Russula* and *Lactarius*, as well as the poisonous Jack O'Lantern, *Omphalotus illudens*, p. 34) also become vase-shaped as they age. The way to tell them from "true" vases is by looking at the underside of the cap. Agarics have sharp-edged, blade-like gills on the underside, while chanterelles and the Lobster have either blunt ridges or a smooth surface.

Chanterelle

(Cantharellus cibarius)

Bright orange to yellow cap with wavy margins; underside with orange-yellow, forked ridges that descend the stalk

David Stonner

Edibility ★★★★ ⚠

CHOICE—with caution. Take care not to confuse chanterelles with the Jack O'Lantern (see Look-alikes). Chanterelles are best preserved by sautéing in butter with a little onion and freezing in zip-lock bags. They are wonderful. (For recipes, see pages 148–150, 161 and 167.)

Season Late June–early August

Habitat Single to many in moss, leaves, and grass, on paths, and under oaks

Cap **Width:** ½–6″ ▪ **Shape:** Convex, becoming flat to funnel shaped, sunken in center, sometimes flower-like ▪ **Color:** Orange to orange-yellow ▪ **Texture:** Smooth

Underside Orange to yellow, with narrow, thick-edged ridges that are forked and cross-veined, and descend the stalk; does not have true gills

Stalk **Length:** 1–3″ ▪ **Width:** ½–1″ ▪ **Shape:** Can be curved or off-center ▪ **Color:** Orange to yellowish to whitish ▪ **Texture:** Smooth ▪ **Other features:** Flesh is white

Spores **Spore print color:** Pinkish-yellow ▪ **Spores magnified:** Elliptical, smooth

Look-alikes The poisonous Jack O'Lantern (*Omphalotus illudens*, p. 34) grows clustered on stumps or buried wood, has close, sharp-edged gills, and fruits in the fall. The Hedgehog (*Hydnum repandum*, p. 122) has a toothed underside. The Smooth Chanterelle (*Cantharellus lateritius*, p. 102) is smooth on the underside.

This is probably the most popular edible mushroom in the world. The habitat for both the Chanterelle and the Smooth Chanterelle (*Cantharellus lateritius*, p. 102) is the same and both are equally delicious. In Missouri, we see more of the Smooth Chanterelle. Some people think that chanterelles smell like apricots.

Cinnabar Chanterelle

(Cantharellus cinnabarinus)

Small, reddish-orange mushroom with forked ridges on the underside that descend the stalk

Jon Rapp

Edibility ★★

Good. Though it doesn't have a lot of flavor, the Cinnabar Chanterelle can add a lovely aesthetic effect when mixed with other chanterelles. (For recipe, see page 168.)

Season Late June—early August

Habitat Single to many in moss, leaves, and grass, on paths, and under oaks

Cap **Width:** ¼–1½″ ▪ **Shape:** Convex, becoming flat, with incurved, wavy margins ▪ **Color:** Reddish-orange, becoming pinkish with age ▪ **Texture:** Smooth

Underside Reddish to pinkish, with thick-edged ridges that are forked and cross-veined, and descend the stalk; does not have true gills

Stalk **Length:** ½–1½″ ▪ **Width:** ¼–½″ ▪ **Shape:** Can be tapering downward and/or off-center ▪ **Color:** Reddish-orange ▪ **Texture:** Smooth

Spores **Spore print color:** Pinkish-cream ▪ **Spores magnified:** Elliptical, smooth

Look-alikes The Scarlet Cup (*Sarcosypha dudlyi*, p. 134) fruits on dead branches and twigs.

The Cinnabar Chanterelle is a very common little mushroom and is often a sign that other chanterelles (*Cantharellus cibarius, C. lateritius*) are around. Keep looking!

Smooth Chanterelle

(Cantharellus lateritius)

Bright orange to yellow cap, wavy margins, smooth on the underside

David Stonner

Edibility ★★★★ ⚠

CHOICE—with caution. Take care not to confuse chanterelles with the Jack O'Lantern (see Look-alikes). The Smooth Chanterelle is best preserved by sautéing in butter with a little onion and freezing in zip-lock bags. They are wonderful! Mmmmm. (For recipes, see pages 148–150, 161 and 167.)

Season Late June–early August

Habitat Single to many to *very many* in moss, leaves, grass, in paths, and under oaks

Cap **Width:** ½–6″ ▪ **Shape:** Convex, becoming flat to funnel shaped, sunken in center, sometimes flower-like ▪ **Color:** Orange to orange-yellow ▪ **Texture:** Smooth

Underside Orange to yellow, smooth or slightly ridged; does not have true gills

Stalk **Length:** 1–3″ ▪ **Width:** ½–1″ ▪ **Shape:** Can be curved or off-center ▪ **Color:** Orange to yellowish to whitish ▪ **Texture:** Smooth ▪ **Other features:** Flesh is white

Spores **Spore print color:** Pinkish-yellow ▪ **Spores magnified:** Elliptical, smooth

Look-alikes The poisonous Jack O'Lantern (*Omphalotus illudens*, p. 34) grows clustered on stumps or buried wood, has close, sharp-edged gills and fruits in the fall. The Hedgehog (*Hydnum repandum*, p. 122) has a toothed underside. The Chanterelle (*Cantharellus cibarius*, p. 100) has forked ridges on the underside.

This chanterelle is very common when in season and you should find lots in Missouri's oak-hickory forests, along with ticks, chiggers and the sweat rolling down your face. The Smooth Chanterelle can be small, tight, and round, or large and flower-like with wavy edges. Either way it is easy to identify. See if you can detect the odor of apricots on a freshly gathered chanterelle.

Black Trumpet

(Craterellus cornucopioides)

Dark brown to black, no gills, vase- or trumpet-shaped, with a wavy margin

Michael Kuo

Edibility ★★★★
CHOICE. The Black Trumpet is best preserved by drying. It is delicious with eggs and beautiful as a garnish for squash soup. (For recipes, see pages 147 and 166.)

Season June–September

Habitat Few to many on rocky, mossy hillsides in deciduous woods

Fruiting Body **Width:** ⅛–3½″ ▪ **Height:** 1–5½″ ▪ **Shape:** Funnel-shaped and hollow, often with wavy margin ▪ **Color:** Upper surface dark brown to black; underside brown to gray when immature, turning salmony when mature ▪ **Texture:** Upper surface dry and scaly, underside smooth to slightly veined

Spores **Spore print color:** Ochre-buff to ochre-orange ▪ **Spores magnified:** Elliptical, smooth, colorless

Look-alikes None in Missouri

The Black Trumpet can be hard to see, because these mushrooms are small and their color blends in nicely with the forest floor. However, when you see one, there will be more. Don't give up!

Also may be called *Craterellus fallax*, Horn of Plenty, Black Chanterelle, or Trumpet of the Dead.

Lobster Mushroom

(Hypomyces lactifluorum)

The cap, gills and stalk of the host mushroom are covered by a bumpy, vivid orange to orange-red layer of mold

David Stonner

Edibility ★★★★
CHOICE. This is a delicious, meaty mushroom. (For recipes, see pages 156 and 160.)

Season July–October

Habitat Single to many, in mixed woods. When not completely up, the Lobster can often be found by looking under bumps in the ground.

Cap, Gills, Stalk The entire host mushroom is covered with a bright orange to orange-red, mold-like parasitic fungus. A mushroom on a mushroom! The surface of the parasite has fine bumps, each of which is a flask-like vessel in which the spores are produced. The gills of the host mushroom can be entirely obscured by the parasite. When cut through, the Lobster is pure white inside, which indicates the color of the host mushroom.

Spores **Spore print:** Clear ▪ **Spores magnified:** Spindle-shaped, strongly warted

Look-alikes The Lobster is very unusual. There are no look-alikes in Missouri.

The bright orange-red parasitic fungus actually transforms an ordinary non-edible white *Lactarius* or *Russula* (possibly a *Russula brevipes* or *Lactarius piperatus*) into an excellent edible mushroom. What a fascinating phenomenon. Mushrooms always amaze me!

Club

(Morels and false morels)

Fungi in the "club" category—otherwise know as morels and false morels—have thick, whitish stalks and bulbous caps, and (with a little imagination) do look like clubs. But really, who identifies morels that way? It's those distinctive pits, ridges, and wrinkles that tell you that you are looking at a true or false morel.

True morels have caps with deep pits and ridges, and look something like a honeycomb or sponge on a stalk. The ridges range in color from light yellow-gray to black.

The caps of false morels are wrinkled and brain-like, or have large, saddle-shaped lobes. They come in shades of reddish-brown.

Both true and false morels always grow on the ground. True morels are a gourmet treat, but false morels can be deadly.

Gabled False Morel

(Gyromitra brunnea)

Reddish-brown, lobed and wrinkled cap, with a whitish stalk stuffed with cottony tissue

Jon Rapp

Edibility

DEADLY. Many Missourians, including whole families, traditionally have eaten and still do eat false morels. However, since serious poisoning and even death is possible, this mushroom is not recommended.

Season
Late March–May

Habitat
Singly or in groups in mixed woods

Cap **Width:** 1½–5″ ▪ **Height:** 2–6″ ▪ **Shape:** Wrinkled, often with large, saddle-shaped lobes ▪ **Color:** Reddish brown outside, buff-tan inside ▪ **Other features:** Cap margin is not fused to the stalk; interior is chambered

Stalk **Length:** 2–5″ ▪ **Width:** 1–4″ ▪ **Shape:** Enlarges toward base ▪ **Color:** Whitish ▪ **Texture:** Grooved to smooth ▪ **Other features:** Stuffed with cottony white tissue

Spores **Spore print color:** Clear to white ▪ **Spores magnified:** Elliptical, smooth

Look-alikes It is said that true morels (*Morchella spp.*) look like false morels, though personally I don't think they do.

The Big Red False Morel (*Gyromitra caroliniana*, p. 107) is more brain-like than the Gabled False Morel, which has large, saddle-shaped lobes. The Big Red False Morel also has a cap margin that is fused to the stalk.

For more information about why you should NOT eat false morels, see page 15.

Big Red False Morel

(Gyromitra caroliniana)

Brad Bomanz

Reddish-brown, convoluted, brain-like cap, with a whitish stalk stuffed with cottony tissue

Edibility

DEADLY. Many Missourians, including whole families, traditionally have eaten and still do eat false morels. However, since serious poisoning and even death is possible, this mushroom is not recommended.

Season Late March–May

Habitat Singly or in groups in mixed woods

Cap **Width:** 1½–7″ ▪ **Height:** 2–10″ ▪ **Shape:** Convoluted, brain-like ▪ **Color:** Reddish brown outside, buff-tan inside ▪ **Other features:** Cap margin is fused to the stalk; interior is chambered

Stalk **Length:** 2–5″ ▪ **Width:** 1–4″ ▪ **Shape:** Enlarges toward base ▪ **Color:** Whitish ▪ **Texture:** Grooved to smooth ▪ **Other features:** Stuffed with cottony white tissue

Spores **Spore print color:** Clear to white ▪ **Spores magnified:** Elliptical, smooth

Look-alikes It is said that true morels (*Morchella spp.*) look like false morels, though personally I don't think so.

The Gabled False Morel (*Gyromitra brunnea*, p. 106) is more lobed and saddle-shaped than brainlike, and has a cap margin that is not fused to the stalk.

For more information about why you should NOT eat false morels, see page 15.

Black Morel

(Morchella elata)

Honeycombed cap with black to brownish-black ridges and yellowish-brown pits; completely hollow

Cliff White

Edibility ★★★★
CHOICE. Simply put, morels are delicious! Sauté them in butter or try them creamed. (For recipe, see page 154.)

Season April and early May

Habitat Single to many on the ground in deciduous woods, disturbed areas and recently burned areas. Especially under white ash; also under tulip poplars, oak, hickory.

Cap **Width:** ½–1½″ ▪ **Height:** ½–2″ ▪ **Shape:** Elongate and conical, with vertically elongated ridges and pits ▪ **Color:** Ridges are black to brownish-black, pits are yellowish-brown ▪ **Texture:** Deeply pitted ▪ **Other features:** Hollow; bottom of cap is fused to the stalk

Stalk **Length:** 2–4″ ▪ **Width:** ½–1½″ ▪ **Shape:** Sometimes enlarged at the base ▪ **Color:** Whitish ▪ **Texture:** Granular ▪ **Other features:** Hollow

Spores **Spore print color:** White to cream ▪ **Spores magnified:** Elliptical, smooth ▪ **Other features:** Located inside the pits

Look-alikes The poisonous false morels (*Gyromitra brunnea*, p. 106, and *G. caroliniana*, p. 107) are reddish and have wrinkled, lobed or brain-shaped caps and dense (not hollow) stalks. The bottom half of the cap of the Half-free Morel (*Morchella semilibera*, p. 110) hangs free from the stalk. The cap of the Yellow Morel (*Morchella esculenta*, p. 109) has yellow to yellow-brown ridges and is more oval.

All true morels are hollow from top to bottom. Make sure that what you have is a true morel—then enjoy.

Recent DNA studies have found that what we in Missouri call the Black Morel probably is not *Morchella elata*, but a different species. Mycology is an ever-evolving science.

Yellow Morel

(Morchella esculenta)

Cliff White

Honeycombed cap with yellow to yellow-gray to yellow-brown ridges and pits; completely hollow

Edibility ★★★★

CHOICE. If you happen to collect more morels than you can eat or give away (we should all have this problem!), drying is a good way to preserve them. A dehydrator works well, but you can also string them and dry them in the sun. Drying intensifies the flavor and odor of the morel, so don't be afraid to experiment. (For recipe, see page 154.)

Season

April and early May

Habitat

Single to many on the ground in deciduous woods, disturbed areas, and recently burned areas. Especially under dying elms, living white ashes and cottonwoods; also under tulip poplars, oaks, hickories.

Cap

Width: 1½–3″ (occasionally much larger) ▪ **Height:** 2½–6″ (occasionally much larger) ▪ **Shape:** Oval to elongate, with vertically elongated ridges and pits ▪ **Color:** Ridges and pits are yellow to yellow-gray to yellow-brown ▪ **Texture:** Deeply pitted ▪ **Other features:** Hollow; bottom of cap is fused to the stalk

Stalk

Length: 1–2″ ▪ **Width:** ½–2″ ▪ **Shape:** Sometimes enlarged at the base ▪ **Color:** Whitish ▪ **Texture:** Ribbed ▪ **Other features:** Hollow

Spores

Spore print color: Creamy yellow to ochre-yellow ▪ **Spores magnified:** Elliptical, smooth ▪ **Other features:** Located inside the pits

Look-alikes

The poisonous false morels (*Gyromitra caroliniana*, p. 107, and *G. brunnea*, p. 106) are reddish and have wrinkled, lobed, or brain-shaped caps and dense (not hollow) stalks. The bottom half of the cap of the Half-free Morel (*Morchella semilibera*, p. 110) hangs free from the stalk. The cap of the Black Morel (*Morchella elata*, p. 108) has black to brownish-black ridges and is more conical.

Sometimes the Yellow Morel is small and grayish. Late in the season it can be very large, up to 12" high and 6" thick.

Half-free Morel

(Morchella semilibera)

Brad Bomanz

Honeycombed cap with brownish-black ridges and yellowish-brown pits; bottom half hanging free from the whitish stalk; completely hollow

Edibility ★★★
Excellent. These morels are definitely worth eating, although their flavor is mild compared to that of the other morels. If you find some half-free morels, you can add them to a batch of yellows and/or blacks. Oh, when will April be here?

Season April

Habitat Scattered in mixed hardwoods

Cap **Width:** ½–1½″ ▪ **Height:** ½–1½″ ▪ **Shape:** Conical, with honeycomb-like ridges and pits ▪ **Color:** Ridges are brownish-black, pits are yellowish-brown ▪ **Texture:** Deeply pitted ▪ **Other features:** Hollow; top half of cap attached to stalk, bottom half hanging free like a skirt

Stalk **Length:** 2–4″ ▪ **Width:** ½–1½″ ▪ **Shape:** Enlarging at the base to 1–2″ ▪ **Color:** Whitish to ivory ▪ **Texture:** Has slight vertical ribs ▪ **Other features:** Hollow

Spores **Spore print color:** Cream to yellowish to orange ▪ **Spores magnified:** Elliptical, smooth ▪ **Other features:** Located inside the pits

Look-alikes The poisonous false morels (*Gyromitra caroliniana*, p. 107, and *G. brunnea*, p. 106) are reddish and have wrinkled, lobed, or brain-shaped caps and dense (not hollow) stalks. The Yellow Morel (*Morchella esculenta*, p. 109) and the Black Morel (*Morchella elata*, p. 108) have larger caps, and the bottom of the cap in both species is fused to the stalk.

The Half-free Morel usually pops up before other morels and can really get your morel adrenaline going!

Ball

(Puffballs, earthstars, *Lycogala*)

If all or part of the fungus you have found is shaped like a ball, it goes in this category.

The "ball" structure is actually a spore sac. When immature, the spore sac is solid inside, but as it matures the inside changes into a mass of powdery spores. The spores puff out from a pore that forms at the top of the sac, or are released when the sac is torn by weathering (or stomped on by humans). Both puffballs and earthstars produce spores this way.

Puffballs are round and leathery, and their surface may be smooth or spiny. Some species stay small, while others can grow to be enormous—the size of a soccer ball, or even larger. Some puffballs are good edibles, but a few are poisonous.

An earthstar looks like a small puffball sitting in the center of a leathery brown star. They are truly fascinating fungi, but not edible. Both puffballs and earthstars grow on the ground or on wood debris.

I have also included the Wolf's Milk Slime (*Lycogala epidendrum*, p. 114) in this group, even though it isn't actually a fungus. This common slime mold looks like little pink balls attached to a log.

Giant Puffball

(Calvatia gigantea)

Tim Gleason

Huge, white, smooth ball with a completely white interior that becomes yellowish-green with age

Edibility ★★★★ ⚠
CHOICE—with caution. Cut open each puffball, from top to bottom, to make sure of your identification (see Look-alikes). Then go ahead and make some Puffball Parmesan! (For recipe, see page 165.)

Season May–October

Habitat Single or many in open pastures, woods, lawns

Fruiting Body **Width:** 8–20″ ▪ **Height:** 8–20″ ▪ **Shape:** Round ▪ **Color:** Outside white; inside pure white when fresh and young, yellowish-green with age ▪ **Texture:** Outside smooth, soft, cracking irregularly; inside marshmallow-like ▪ **Other features:** Root-like attachment at base

Spores **Spore print color:** Greenish-brown ▪ **Spores magnified:** Round

Look-alikes Some other types of white mushrooms, including the deadly Destroying Angel (*Amanita bisporigera*, p. 39), have stages in which they could be mistaken for a puffball. Make sure you cut through the Giant Puffball from top to bottom to confirm that it is pure white inside, like a marshmallow, with no sign of a cap or stem.

A Giant Puffball can be very large—sometimes as big as a soccer ball.

Earthstar

(Geastrum spp.)

Roundish ball in the center of star-like rays.

Edibility ✕
Not Edible

Season July–September

Habitat In the strangest places, but mostly single to several on the floor of open woods

Fruiting Body Star-shaped; composed of a ball (spore sac) surrounded by 4–10 rays, depending on the species. Ball up to 1½″ wide, with an opening or hole at the top. Rays ½–2″ long. Entire mushroom is grayish-brown.

Spores **Spore print color:** Brown ▪ **Spores magnified:** Round, warted

Look-alikes None in Missouri

You will know when you have found an Earthstar, because no other mushroom looks like it. Missouri has a few different *Geastrum* species, but for our purposes the name Earthstar will do. I think they are a magically beautiful creation. If you should find one, take it home and let it dry. It will make a good keepsake (and conversation piece) and will last forever.

Wolf's-milk Slime

(Lycogala epidendrum)

Little, round, reddish-pink balls, exuding a pinkish-gray paste when popped

Edibility ✕
Not Edible

Season June–November

Habitat In groups on dead wood, especially large logs

Fruiting Body **Width and Height:** ⅓–⅝″ ▪ **Shape:** Round, with an opening at the top ▪ **Color:** Outside reddish-pink when young, becoming tannish-olive with age; inside pinkish-gray, becoming ochre with age ▪ **Texture:** Outside smooth; inside paste-like, becoming powdery with age

Spores **Spore print color:** Pinkish-gray to ochre ▪ **Spores magnified:** Round, netted

Look-alikes None in Missouri

The Wolf's-milk Slime looks like a tiny reddish-pink puffball. Before it is fully mature, you can pop it and a pinkish-gray substance, with the texture of toothpaste, will ooze out. Also called Toothpaste Slime.

Slime Molds, or Myxomycetes, aren't actually fungi—they are a group of fungus-like organisms which at one time were regarded as animals, then thought to be plants, then fungi. Now, because of DNA studies, slime molds are believed to be closer to the protozoa. They are studied by botanists and mycologists. I included the Wolf's-milk Slime in this book because it is really interesting and mushroom hunters tend to see it a lot.

Gem-studded Puffball

(Lycoperdon perlatum)

Noppadol Paothong

White, roundish to turban-shaped ball, densely covered with spiny warts, with a pore at the top

Edibility ★★★ ⚠

Excellent, when young and fresh—with caution. Cut open each puffball from top to bottom to make sure of your identification (see Look-alikes).

Season July–October

Habitat Singly or in clusters on the ground in open woods, along roads, in waste areas

Fruiting Body

Width: 1–2½" ▪ **Height:** 1–3" ▪ **Shape:** Roundish to turban-shaped with an elongated base ▪ **Color:** Outside white, becoming yellowish-pinkish-brownish; inside pure white, becoming brownish dust ▪ **Texture:** Covered with spiny, detachable warts, especially dense at the top ▪ **Other features:** When mature, the pore opening at the top releases spores which look like thick dust

Spores

Spore print color: Olive-brownish ▪ **Spores magnified:** Elongated, stalk-like

Look-alikes

The poisonous Pigskin Puffball (*Scleroderma citrinum*, p. 117) is brownish, and when cut through is dark brownish-purple on the inside. The edible Pear-shaped Puffball (*Lycoperdon pyriforme*, p. 116) is brownish, with a smoother surface, and fruits on decaying wood.

Some other types of white mushrooms, including the deadly Destroying Angel (*Amanita bisporigera*, p. 39), have stages in which they could be mistaken for a puffball. Make sure you cut through the Gem-studded Puffball from top to bottom to confirm that it is pure white inside, like a marshmallow, with no sign of a cap or stem.

Gem-studded Puffballs are very common and tasty mushrooms. However, to get a decent meal out of them you'd have to pick lots!

Pear-shaped Puffball

(Lycoperdon pyriforme)

Cliff White

Pear-shaped, yellowish-brownish puffball with pore at the top

Edibility ★★★ ⚠
Excellent, when young and fresh—with caution. Cut open each puffball from top to bottom to make sure of your identification (see Look-alikes).

Season July–November

Habitat In large clusters on decaying wood, logs and stumps

Fruiting Body **Width:** ½–1½″ ▪ **Height:** ½–1¾″ ▪ **Shape:** Pear-shaped ▪ **Color:** Outside yellowish-brownish; inside pure white ▪ **Texture:** Surface has tiny warts ▪ **Other features:** Attached to wood by strands of mycelium. When the fruiting body is mature, the pore opening at the top releases spores.

Spores **Spore print color:** Olive brown ▪ **Spores magnified:** Round, smooth

Look-alikes The poisonous Pigskin Puffball (*Scleroderma citrinum*, p. 117) is brownish, and when cut open is dark brownish-purple inside. The edible Gem-studded Puffball (*Lycoperdon perlatum*, p. 115) is white with dense spiny warts, and fruits on the ground rather than on wood.

Some other types of white mushrooms, including the deadly Destroying Angel (*Amanita bisporigera*, p. 39), have stages in which they could be mistaken for a puffball. Make sure you cut through the Pear-shaped Puffball from top to bottom to confirm that it is pure white inside, like a marshmallow, with no sign of a cap or stem.

In Greek, "*pyriforme*" means pear-shaped, so one common name of *Lycoperdon pyriforme* is the Pear-shaped Puffball. But this mushroom has another, less polite common name. In Greek, "*lyco*" means wolf, and "*perdon*" means to break wind. So another name for *Lycoperdon pyriforme* is the Wolf-fart Puffball. No kidding!

Pigskin Puffball

(Scleroderma citrinum)

Roundish, warted, yellowish-brown ball with blackish-purple flesh

Edibility ☠
POISONOUS. This puffball can cause upset stomach, nausea and vomiting.

Season July–October

Habitat Single to many on the ground, on wood debris, near trees in woods

Fruiting Body **Width:** 1–6″ ▪ **Height:** 1–6″ ▪ **Shape:** Roundish to flattened ▪ **Color:** Outside yellowish-brown. When cut through, the inside is light (not white), becoming marbled, becoming purplish, becoming blackish with age ▪ **Texture:** Leathery, thick-skinned, with coarse scales or warts ▪ **Other features:** With a pore at the top

Spores **Spore print color:** Blackish-brown ▪ **Spores magnified:** Round, ornamented

Look-alikes The edible Pear-shaped Puffball (*Lycoperdon pyriforme*, p. 116) and Gem-studded Puffball (*Lycoperdon perlatum*, p. 115) are white on the inside when cut through.

I don't think you'll confuse this with an edible puffball, as the Pigskin Puffball has a thick rind-like skin and is never pure white on the inside.

Tooth

(Tooth fungi)

Any mushroom with pointed spines or "teeth" on the underside of the cap, or all over its surface, is a tooth fungus. Some tooth fungi grow on the ground, some on living or dead trees. They may grow singly or in groups. None are known to be poisonous, and a few are very good edibles—like the three described here.

Comb Tooth

(Hericium coralloides)

Branched, whitish mass on decaying deciduous trees; branches covered with tufts of hanging, toothlike spines

Jon Rapp

Edibility ★★★★

CHOICE. The Comb Tooth is tasty only when young and fresh. It gets sour and bitter as it matures. (For recipe, see page 158.)

Season August–October

Habitat Single to several on fallen logs and decaying deciduous trees

Fruiting Body **Width:** 4–10″ ▪ **Height:** 3–6″ ▪ **Shape:** Irregular mass with multiple branches; sides and undersurfaces of branches covered with tufts of hanging, tooth-like spines, each spine ¼–1″ long ▪ **Color:** White to creamy, becoming yellowish ▪ **Texture:** Coarsely toothed, yet soft

Stalk **Length:** Short ▪ **Width:** Thick ▪ **Shape:** Stublike, dividing into spine-covered branches ▪ **Color:** White to creamy, becoming yellowish ▪ **Texture:** Hairy

Spores **Spore print color:** White ▪ **Spores magnified:** Almost round, smooth to roughened, colorless

Look-alikes The Bearded Tooth (*Hericium erinaceus*, p. 121) is an unbranched, beard-like mass of long, hanging spines, and fruits on living trees.

We tend to look only down when hunting for mushrooms. Try looking up–on the trunks of trees. Who knows what you might find!

The Comb Tooth was previously called *Hericium ramosum.*

Bearded Tooth

(Hericium erinaceus)

Beard-like, whitish mass on living deciduous trees

Jon Rapp

Edibility ★★★★
CHOICE. The Bearded Tooth is tasty only when young and fresh. It gets sour and bitter as it matures. Try Hericium Salad, a great imitation of crab meat salad (for recipe, see page 158).

Season August–November

Habitat Single, on trunks of living deciduous trees and on fallen trees and logs

Fruiting Body **Width and Height:** 3–10″ ▪ **Shape:** Round, unbranched mass of long, hanging, tooth-like spines, each ½–2″ long; spines hanging evenly from a central base ▪ **Color:** White, becoming yellowish ▪ **Texture:** Smooth

Stalk Not present

Spores **Spore print color:** White ▪ **Spores magnified:** Almost round, smooth to roughened with dots, colorless

Look-alikes The Comb Tooth (*Hericium coralloides*, p. 120) has multiple branches covered with tufts of short spines, and fruits on decaying trees.

The Bearded Tooth is sometimes called Lion's Mane, or the Hedgehog Mushroom. Just to add a little confusion, *Hydnum repandum* (p. 122) is also called the Hedgehog. Although they both have spines, they are very different-looking mushrooms.

Hedgehog

(Hydnum repandum)

Irregularly shaped, dull orangish-tan cap; underside with spines or "teeth"

David Stonner

Edibility ★★★★ CHOICE. The Hedgehog has a sweet, nutty flavor and a nice, chewy texture. Older specimens may be a bit bitter.

Season July–November

Habitat Scattered or in groups, on the ground in mixed woods

Cap **Width:** ½–7″ ▪ **Shape:** Convex, becoming flat with a central depression ▪ **Color:** Orangish-tan ▪ **Texture:** Fairly smooth ▪ **Other features:** Margin curves in at first, becoming wavy; flesh is white, bruising ochre

Underside Pale yellowish-white, bruising ochre; covered with spines or "teeth" that descend the stalk

Stalk **Length:** 1–4″ ▪ **Width:** ⅜–1¼″ ▪ **Shape:** Straight ▪ **Color:** Pale yellowish-white ▪ **Texture:** Smooth ▪ **Other features:** Often off-center

Spores **Spore print color:** White ▪ **Spores magnified:** Round, smooth, colorless

Look-alikes Chanterelles (*Cantharellus cibarius*, p. 100, *C. lateritius*, p. 102) do not have "teeth" on their undersides.

The Hedgehog is easy to identify because of the spines or "teeth" on the underside of the cap. Also called *Dentinum repandum.*

Coral

(Coral fungi, *Tremellodendron*)

Coral-shaped fungi can look almost exactly like underwater corals. They are branched and pronged, and even come in beautiful colors—from pale cream to bright orange to vibrant purple.

True coral mushrooms grow mostly on the ground and occasionally on logs and stumps. Although some are edible, they are not among my favorites. A few coral species may make you a bit queasy, but none are seriously poisonous.

As you can guess from its name, the Jellied False Coral (*Tremellodendron pallidum*, p. 125) is not a true coral, but a jelly fungus. However, it looks much more like coral than jelly!

Crown-tipped Coral

(Artomyces pyxidatus)

Cliff White

Many-branched, coral-like mushroom, yellowish-tan, with crown-like tips

Edibility ★ ⚠
Edible—with caution (see Look-alikes).

Season June–September

Habitat Single to several on dead wood of deciduous trees

Fruiting Body **Width:** ¾–2½″ ▪ **Height:** 2–5″ ▪ **Shape:** Branched, usually in 3-sided groupings, with crown-like tips ▪ **Color:** Yellowish, becoming tannish or pinkish ▪ **Texture:** Tough ▪ **Other features:** Very short, thin stalk

Spores **Spore print color:** White ▪ **Spores magnified:** Elliptical, smooth, colorless

Look-alikes Other corals, some of which may cause gastrointestinal upset

An important clue for identifying a Crown-tipped Coral is that it is one of the few corals that grow on wood. Also, if you take a tiny taste, it will be peppery. The crown-like tips are another identifying feature. Think of a castle!

Previously called *Clavicorona pyxidata*.

Jellied False Coral

(Tremellodendron pallidum)

Jon Rapp

Branching, whitish, leathery, coral-like jelly fungus

Edibility ✕
Not Edible. Though the Jellied False Coral can be safely eaten, I think its taste just isn't worth the effort!

Season May–November

Habitat Single or scattered, on the ground in deciduous or mixed woods.

Fruiting Body **Width:** 2–6″ ▪ **Height:** 1–4″ ▪ **Shape:** Coral-like cluster of vertical branches that are often flattened or fused ▪ **Color:** Whitish ▪ **Texture:** Tough but gelatinous

Spores **Spore print color:** White ▪ **Spores magnified:** Sausage-shaped, smooth

Look-alikes The Jellied False Coral could be confused with many true corals. However, true coral mushrooms are brittle and break easily, while the Jellied False Coral is tough, not brittle.

Because the Jellied False Coral is so tough and leathery, spring fruiting of this jelly fungus may persist throughout the summer and fall.

Column
(Stinkhorns, earth tongues)

"Column" mushrooms are almost all stalk. They may have small heads shaped like wrinkled balls, cones, or tongues, or they may just taper to a point. The stalks may be straight, curved or crooked.

This category includes stinkhorns and earth tongues, which are pretty odd fungi. Stinkhorns are notorious for their suggestive shape and awful smell. The top of the stalk is covered with a foul, greenish slime, which attracts flies. Earth tongues are little wormlike things that don't attract much notice. One possible exception is Dead Man's Fingers (*Xylaria polymorpha*, p. 130). The mature fruiting bodies of this fungus do look, rather horribly, like their name.

Elegant Stinkhorn

(Mutinus elegans)

David Stonner

Long, tapered, pinkish-orange column with a greenish-brown, smelly slime covering the top and a white cup around the base

Edibility ★★ ⚠

Good—with caution. The immature stage of the Elegant Stinkhorn is a white, rubbery "egg" or "button." In this "egg" stage, the Elegant Stinkhorn doesn't have a foul odor and is reported to be edible and quite good. It's also a fun conversation piece! ("Hey, honey, want to have stinkhorn eggs for dinner tonight?") However, if you want to try eating stinkhorn eggs, have an expert identify them, since the deadly amanitas also have an immature "egg" stage. (For recipe, see page 164.)

Season July–September

Habitat On leafy debris, mulch piles, rotting wood; in woods and fields

Fruiting Body Cylindrical, hollow column, ½–1" wide and 4–7" high, pinkish-orange, tapering toward the top; top covered with a slimy, greenish-brown, unpleasant-smelling spore mass, with a small opening at the tip; base enclosed in a white, sac-like cup that is attached to the ground by a white, cord-like tissue

Spores **Spore color:** Greenish-brown ▪ **Spores magnified:** Elliptical, smooth

Look-alikes None in Missouri. This is a very unusual mushroom, and once you see it you'll always remember it. Stinkhorn "eggs," however, require caution (see Edibility).

The Elegant Stinkhorn can emerge from its "egg" and grow to full size (and stinkiness) in just a few hours.

Mutinus elegans is very similar to another stinkhorn, *Mutinus caninus*. Recent research indicates that they may, in fact, be the same species.

Ravenel's Stinkhorn

(Phallus ravenelii)

Long, whitish column with a greenish, smelly slime covering the top and a whitish-pinkish cup around the base

Brad Bomanz

Edibility ★★ ⚠

Good—with caution. The immature stage of the Ravenel's Stinkhorn is a white, rubbery "egg" or "button," about 2 inches wide. In this "egg" stage, the Ravenel's Stinkhorn does not have a foul odor and is known to be edible and quite good. However, don't try to give any to your neighbors as they will think you've finally gone over the edge! Also, a note of caution: If you want to try eating stinkhorn eggs, have an expert identify them, since the deadly amanitas also have an immature "egg" stage. (For recipe, see page 164.)

Season August–October

Habitat Singly to clustered on wood debris, rotted stumps, and sawdust, and in deciduous woods

Fruiting Body Cylindrical column, 1–2" wide and 4–9" high, whitish; top covered with a thick, slimy, greenish-brown, unpleasant smelling, conical spore mass, with a small opening at the tip; base enclosed in a whitish-pinkish, sac-like cup that is attached to the ground by white, cord-like tissue.

Spores **Spore color:** Greenish-brown ▪ **Spores magnified:** Elliptical, smooth, colorless

Look-alikes This is a very unusual mushroom and once you see—and smell—it, you'll always remember it. Stinkhorn "eggs," however, require caution (see Edibility). *Phallus impudicus* (not in this book) has a deeply pitted head.

The strong odor of stinkhorns can be smelled from several feet away. This odor comes from the sticky spore mass on the top of the cap, which flies eat and then disperse.

Dead Man's Fingers

(Xylaria polymorpha)

Black, distorted, club- or finger-shaped fungus with a wrinkled, carbon-like surface

Jon Rapp

Jon Rapp

Edibility ✕
Not Edible

Season June–October, but can be found all year

Habitat In clusters at the base of rotting deciduous wood and stumps

Fruiting Body **Width:** ½–1¼″ ▪ **Height:** ½–3″ ▪ **Shape:** Irregularly club- or finger-shaped, short-stalked ▪ **Color:** Black, carbon-like ▪ **Texture:** Finely wrinkled or roughened surface

Spores **Spore print color:** Dark brown to black ▪ **Spores magnified:** Narrow, spindle-shaped, flat on one side

Look-alikes Other *Xylaria* species; also the very young Devil's Urn (*Urnula craterium*, p. 136), before the cup has opened, when it is much softer

In the spring, Dead Man's Fingers may be covered with white, powdery spores that become black as the mushroom matures. This is an eerie, unusual-looking mushroom—there is nothing quite like it.

Cup

(Cup fungi, bird's nest fungi)

Fungi in this category don't have caps, gills or pores, and often have no stalks. Basically they just look like small cups, bowls, or urns.

Most species of cup-shaped fungi are simply called—you guessed it—"cup fungi." Some are large enough to be found easily, others are tiny and cute, and many are colorful. The spores of cup fungi line the inner surface of the cup, ready to puff or float out. Their flesh is brittle, and they break easily.

Other species of cup-shaped fungi are called bird's nest fungi, because they look like tiny nests with eggs. The "eggs" are actually spore sacs, which distribute spores when they are splashed out of the "nest" by raindrops.

Both of these groups of cup-shaped fungi grow on the ground or on wood debris. They are not edible, but they are always fun to find.

Splash Cup

(Cyathus striatus)

Small brown cup with tiny "eggs" that are each attached to the "nest" by a cord

David Stonner

Edibility ✕
Not Edible

Season July–October

Habitat Clustered on dead wood, debris, wood chips, mulch

Cup **Width:** ¼–⅝" ▪ **Height:** ¼–⅝" ▪ **Shape:** Small cup, flared at the top, with tiny "eggs" inside ▪ **Color:** Dark brownish-gray ▪ **Texture:** Fluted or striated ▪ **Other features:** Each "egg" 1/32–1/16" wide, flattened, attached to cup by a very thin but strong cord

Spores **Spore print color:** Colorless ▪ **Spores magnified:** Elliptical, smooth, notched at one end

Look-alikes Other small mushrooms that look like bird's nests

The Splash Cup has flaring sides so that rain drops can hit the "eggs"—which are really spore sacs—and dislodge the spores, thereby dispersing them. Pretty remarkable!

The Splash Cup and other little cup mushrooms with "eggs" are commonly called bird's nest fungi.

Hairy Rubber Cup

(Galiella rufa)

Cup-like mushroom, inner surface reddish-brownish, outer surface blackish-brown and hairy

David Stonner

Edibility ✕
Not Edible

Season July–September

Habitat Clustered on deciduous wood

Cup **Width:** ¾–1¼″ ▪ **Shape:** Closed and urn-shaped when immature, then opening to shallow cup ▪ **Color:** Outer surface blackish-brown and hairy; inner surface reddish to chocolate-brown ▪ **Texture:** Tough and rubbery

Stalk (If present) **Length:** ⅜–¾″ ▪ **Width:** ¼–⅝″ ▪ **Shape:** Thick ▪ **Color:** Blackish-brown ▪ **Texture:** Has a dense covering of hairs

Spores **Spore print color:** Reddish-brown ▪ **Spores magnified:** Elliptical, with narrow ends and tiny warts

Look-alikes The Devil's Urn (*Urnula craterium*, p. 136) has a blackish inner surface and fruits in the spring.

The Hairy Rubber Cup sometimes can be found on sticks and small logs. Its flesh is rubbery and gelatinous and sometimes squishy.

Scarlet Cup

(Sarcoscypha dudleyi)

Tiny, red, usually stalkless cup with a white outer surface

Joe McFarland

Edibility ✕
Not Edible

Season March–May

Habitat Scattered on fallen wet sticks and branches in damp deciduous woods

Cup **Width:** ¾–1½" ▪ **Height:** ¾–1¼" ▪ **Shape:** Shallow cup ▪ **Color:** Outer surface is white, inner surface is scarlet ▪ **Texture:** Outer surface has tiny hairs

Stalk (If present) **Length:** Short ▪ **Width:** Thick ▪ **Shape:** Equal ▪ **Color:** White

Spores **Spore print color:** Whitish-cream ▪ **Spores magnified:** Elliptical, smooth

Look-alikes The Stalked Scarlet Cup (*Sarcoscypha occidentalis*, p. 135) has a well-developed stalk and a smaller cup. It appears later in the season than the Scarlet Cup. The Cinnabar Chanterelle (*Cantharellus cinnabarinus*, p. 101) grows on the ground.

In early spring, when the woods are still brown, look on twigs and branches for the bright-red Scarlet Cup.

Stalked Scarlet Cup

(Sarcoscypha occidentalis)

Tiny red cup on a tiny white stalk

David Stonner

Edibility ✕
Not Edible

Season May–June, later in cooler years

Habitat Scattered on fallen wet sticks and branches in damp deciduous woods

Cup **Width:** ¼–⅝″ ▪ **Height:** ⅜″ ▪ **Shape:** Shallow cup ▪ **Color:** Outer surface is white, inner surface is scarlet ▪ **Texture:** Outer surface is smooth

Stalk **Length:** ⅜–1¼″ ▪ **Width:** 1⁄16″ ▪ **Shape:** Equal ▪ **Color:** White

Spores **Spore print color:** Whitish-cream ▪ **Spores magnified:** Elliptical, smooth, with one drop of oil at each end

Look-alikes The Scarlet Cup (*Sarcoscypha dudleyi*, p. 134) has a larger cup and either a very short stalk or none at all. It appears earlier in the season than the Stalked Scarlet Cup.

Though it is often overlooked, the Stalked Scarlet Cup is easily identified by its bright red color, tiny white stalk, and very small size. It's a cutie!

Devil's Urn

(Urnula craterium)

Urn-shaped, leathery brown cup

Edibility ✕
Not Edible

Season March–May

Habitat Clustered on small to medium-sized decaying branches of hardwoods. They especially like fallen branches of oak trees.

Cup **Width:** 1¾–3¼″ ▪ **Height:** 1½–2½″ ▪ **Shape:** Closed when immature, then opening to a deep cup ▪ **Color:** Inner and outer surfaces are dark brownish-black ▪ **Texture:** Tough and rubbery

Stalk **Length:** 1¼–1¾″ ▪ **Width:** ¼″ ▪ **Shape:** Thick, equal ▪ **Color:** Blackish ▪ **Texture:** Has a dense covering of hairs

Spores **Spore print color:** Blackish-brown ▪ **Spores magnified:** Elliptical, smooth

Look-alikes The Hairy Rubber Cup (*Galiella rufa*, p. 133) fruits July-September, and its inner surface is chocolate brown. Before the Devil's Urn has opened, it may look like the Dead Man's Fingers (*Xylaria polymorpha*, p. 130).

When the Devil's Urn is mature, it is a good sign that morels are popping! Look around—morels may be right under your feet!

Jelly

(Jelly fungi)

Jelly fungi are translucent, irregular blobs that look and feel like jelly or rubber. They may have short stalks, or be directly attached to wood.

Some jelly fungi have appealing colors—especially the bright-yellow Witches' Butter (*Tremella mesenterica*, p. 141). They grow mostly on wood, but sometimes on the ground. A few jellies are edible, and none are known to be poisonous.

Wood Ear

or Tree Ear
(Auricularia auricula-judae)

Reddish-brown to grayish-black, rubbery, ear or cup-shaped mushroom

Patrick Harvey

Edibility ★ ℞
Edible/Medicinal. A related species is cultivated in Asia and sold in the U.S. in Asian markets. You may have eaten it in Chinese hot and sour soup.

Season May–November

Habitat Usually in groups on rotting wood

Fruiting Body **Width:** 1–6″ ▪ **Shape:** Ear or cup-shaped ▪ **Color:** Upper surface reddish-brown to grayish to blackish; underside often lighter than the upper surface ▪ **Texture:** Upper surface smooth, wavy; underside silky or finely hairy, irregularly veined; flesh thin and rubbery

Spores **Spore print color:** White ▪ **Spores magnified:** Sausage-shaped, smooth, colorless

Look-alikes The Wood Ear could be confused with a cup fungus except that it is rubbery, not brittle like many cup fungi, and can be found in many irregular shapes.

The Wood Ear has been reported to positively affect blood coagulation and decrease blood cholesterol levels. Since it is a very popular edible mushroom in China, it may contribute to the low incidence of heart disease there.

Pale Jelly Roll

(Exidia alba)

Small, white, gelatinous mass; shape irregular, jelly-like to brain-like

David Stonner

Edibility ✕

Not Edible

Season Spring and fall

Habitat Clustered on dead wood of deciduous trees

Fruiting Body **Width:** 3⁄8–3⁄4"

▪ **Shape:** Irregular; may look like a blob of jelly or a blister, or appear cup-like or brain-like; fruiting bodies may fuse and form rows ▪ **Color:** White ▪ **Texture:** Gelatinous, smooth

Spores **Spore print color:** White ▪ **Spores magnified:** Sausage-shaped, smooth

Look-alikes Other "jellies" in the *Exidia* genus—except for their colors, which can be black, reddish-brown or amber. Witches' Butter (*Tremella mesenterica*, p. 141) is yellow in color.

If you see a "jelly," you'll sound smart by saying "It's in the *Exidia* genus, but I'm not sure of the species."

Jelly Baby

(Leotia lubrica)

Small mushroom with a gelatinous, ochre-yellow stalk and head

Michael Kuo

Edibility ✕
Not Edible

Season July–October

Habitat In groups on soil in mixed woods

Head **Width:** ½–1½″ ▪ **Shape:** Convoluted, with an inrolled margin ▪ **Color:** Ochre-yellow with an olive tint ▪ **Texture:** Gelatinous, smooth

Stalk **Length:** ¾–2″ ▪ **Width:** ¼–½″ ▪ **Shape:** Cylindrical, hollow ▪ **Color:** Ochre-yellow ▪ **Texture:** Can have tiny scales

Spores **Spore print color:** Transparent ▪ **Spores magnified:** Spindle-shaped

Look-alikes Other jellies, but this color is unique

Jelly Babies often can be found in large clusters. They are cute little things!

Witches' Butter

(Tremella mesenterica)

Small, yellow, irregularly-lobed, gelatinous mass

David Stonner

Edibility ★
Edible. Witches' Butter can be used in cooking as an addition to soups and stews. It has little flavor but the texture and color may be appealing.

Season Year-round

Habitat In masses on dead, deciduous wood, especially oaks

Fruiting Body **Width:** 1–3″ ▪ **Height:** 1¼–1⅝″ ▪ **Shape:** Irregularly lobed, brain-like ▪ **Color:** Sulfur-yellow to pale yellow ▪ **Texture:** Gelatinous ▪ **Other features:** Trembles at the slightest touch

Spores **Spore print color:** Yellowish ▪ **Spores magnified:** Oval, elliptical, smooth

Look-alikes Other yellowish "jellies," none of which are known to be poisonous. The Pale Jelly Roll (*Exidia alba*, p. 139) can be similar in size and shape, but is white in color.

Witches' Butter is sometimes found during a warm winter thaw.

Steve Adams

SECTION III

Cookery

Many people in Missouri think that morels are the only edible wild mushrooms in the state. They don't realize that there are lots and lots of other delicious edible mushrooms right here in our beautiful Missouri woods, and often right in our own backyards! I hope the 24 recipes in this section will inspire you to try cooking not only morels (which of course are superb) but also some of Missouri's other mushroom treats. The recipes include appetizers, soups, salads, entrees and even a dessert. All are great ways to celebrate Missouri's mushroom bounty.

Morchella esculenta, p. 109

Maxine Stone

Wild Mushroom Cooking Basics

Again, before you decide to cook and eat a mushroom, be SURE of its identification and that it is a safe mushroom to eat. The first time you eat any wild mushroom, please put a few aside in the refrigerator so that if someone has an allergic or poisonous reaction, an expert can make a clear identification and the correct remedy can be used. Also, wild mushrooms should never be eaten raw. They can be difficult to digest, and may contain toxins that are destroyed by cooking.

That being said, all wild mushrooms should be cooked and eaten immediately or preserved for later use. The sooner they are cooked the better, though some mushrooms will last for a few days in the refrigerator stored in a container that lets in air and moisture. I put my mushrooms in a glass or plastic bowl with a damp towel over the top. This seems to work best.

Before cooking, most mushrooms should be cut in half from top to bottom or torn apart, and then checked for insects. Wash only those mushrooms that are dirty or have bugs. Mushrooms are mostly water, so adding more water during cooking is unnecessary.

The following pages contain recipes for a variety of edible wild mushrooms. However, if you have found a lot of one kind of mushroom—maybe some chanterelles or a nice Chicken of the Woods, maybe some blewits or lobsters—I suggest that you first try this basic recipe. Just sauté your mushrooms in butter with a little salt and pepper. You could add onion, garlic, or shallots as desired. Cook on low heat until the natural moisture from the mushrooms is given off, then evaporated. You can eat this fabulous concoction right out of the pan, scooped up with bread or sauced over pasta. This will give you an understanding of the true flavor of your mushroom. Enjoy!

Preserving Wild Mushrooms

Most mushrooms dry well. Mushrooms can be dried in a food dehydrator or in a barely warm oven. They also can be laid outside on a screen or strung and hung to dry in the sun. Dry them until they are hard and not pliable, as this will keep them from decaying. These can be kept in an airtight container for a very long time. To use, rehydrate in warm water for 30–60 minutes. Don't forget to keep the water for future use in soup or another dish. Some mushrooms, like chanterelles, may become a bit rubbery after they are dried. If this should happen, they can be ground to a powder in a coffee or spice mill and used as a seasoning.

For mushrooms like chanterelles that don't dry well, try this method. After cleaning, cook them up with a little butter, onion, salt and pepper until all of the water given off is evaporated. Put them in small zip-lock bags and store in the freezer. They are ready to use as needed. I use this method for chanterelles, and for Hen of the Woods and Chicken of the Woods.

Mushrooms also can be pickled. Though this does preserve the mushroom, it doesn't preserve the flavor very well, as they tend to take on the flavor of the pickling solution.

Recipes

Barley and Blewit Salad

by Maxine Stone
Servings: 4
Oven: 350°

1 cup pearl barley
2 cups fresh blewits (*Lepista nuda*, p. 33) sliced
3–4 cloves garlic, chopped
¼ cup plus 1 tablespoon extra virgin olive oil
2 tablespoons red wine vinegar
2 tablespoons tamari
1 teaspoon Dijon mustard
Salt and pepper
½ teaspoon ground cumin
4 tablespoons toasted sunflower seeds
¼ cup chopped parsley
¼ cup chopped thyme
4 cups torn savoy cabbage

Jon Rapp

Lepista nuda, p. 33

1 Cook barley in water according to directions—usually about an hour. Drain.

2 Combine mushrooms, garlic and 1 tablespoon olive oil in a large pan and roast in the oven for about 15 minutes, stirring occasionally. When mushrooms are cooked and garlic is soft, remove from oven and set aside.

3 Make dressing of ¼ cup olive oil, vinegar, tamari, mustard, salt and pepper, and cumin. Mix well.

4 In a bowl, combine warm cooked barley and remaining ingredients. Drizzle with dressing and serve warm or at room temperature.

What a fantastic way to serve your fresh blewits!

Butternut Squash Soup with Black Trumpets

by Maxine Stone
Servings: 8

Steve Adams

A handful of dried black trumpets
(*Craterellus cornucopioides*, p. 103)
4 pounds butternut squash (about 2)
1½ cup onion, chopped
1 cup celery, sliced
2 tablespoons plus 1 tablespoon butter
2 tablespoons ginger root, grated
½ teaspoon curry powder
½ teaspoon ground cardamom
Dash cayenne powder
Bay leaf (optional)
1 sprig thyme (optional)
Salt and pepper
¼–½ cup dry sherry
Vegetable or chicken stock
¼ cup sour cream or thick Greek yogurt

1 Soak black trumpets in warm water until soft, about ½ hour.

2 Microwave or roast butternut squash, then peel, seed, and cube.

3 Sauté the onion and celery in 2 tablespoons butter until clear, about 5–10 minutes. Add the ginger root, curry, cardamom, cayenne, bay leaf, and thyme, and salt and pepper to taste. Sauté for a minute or two. Add the sherry. Add the squash and enough stock to just cover the squash. Simmer for 20–30 minutes.

4 While the soup is simmering, squeeze water out of black trumpets. Sauté in 1 tablespoon butter for a few minutes. Add salt and pepper to taste.

5 Remove bay leaf and thyme from soup. With an immersible blender, blend soup right in pot (or use a regular blender or food processor). Leave a bit chunky. Ladle into bowls. Put a dollop of sour cream or yogurt in the center and sprinkle a few black trumpets on top.

This is beautiful and delicious.

Chanterelle and Bacon Pizza

by Patrick Harvey
Servings: 3–4
Oven: 450°

1 pizza crust (home-made or ready-to-use)
6 strips bacon
2 tablespoons olive oil
3 cloves fresh garlic, minced
2 shallots, diced
¾ cup chanterelles (*Cantharellus cibarius*, p. 100, or *C. lateritius*, p. 102) measured fresh or rehydrated
½ cup pasta sauce
1 cup fresh mozzarella cheese, torn into pieces
¼ cup freshly grated parmesan cheese
1 teaspoon Italian seasoning
A few leaves of fresh basil, coarsely chopped

"The chants REALLY go well with the bacon."

1 Prepare pizza crust as directed. Fry bacon crisp and drain. Pour off bacon grease and add olive oil to the pan. Add garlic and shallots. Sauté until soft. Add torn chanterelles, and sauté 5 minutes or until done.

2 Spread pasta sauce on pizza crust, arrange bacon slices over sauce, place chanterelles mixture over bacon. Cover with mozzarella and sprinkle parmesan, Italian seasoning and basil over all. Bake for 15 minutes, or until done.

David Stonner

Cantharellus cibarius, p. 100

Chanterelle and Polenta Foil Packs

by David Yates
Servings: 4

2 cups fresh chanterelles (*Cantharellus cibarius*, p. 100, or *C. lateritius*, p. 102)
2 tablespoons butter
Salt and pepper
1 tablespoon olive oil
1 polenta log, purchased
4 sprigs rosemary

Steve Adams

1 Clean chanterelles and tear into bite-size pieces, leaving the very small ones whole. Sauté in butter with salt and pepper to taste for about 4–5 minutes or until liquid is evaporated off.

2 Cut four 12″ x 12″ squares of aluminum foil. Lightly oil each piece. Place a slice or two of polenta on foil. Top with chanterelles and a rosemary sprig. Fold up foil and bake over hot coals for about 10 minutes, or a bit longer if you prefer the polenta edges crunchy!

This is **great camping food.** A little gourmet and a lot delicious. This dish works just as well at home, in a 425 degree oven.

Chanterelle and Potato Soup

by Donna Harvey
Servings: 4

2 large gold potatoes, peeled and cubed
½–1 cup chanterelles (*Cantharellus cibarius*, p. 100, or *C. lateritius*, p. 102), torn
2 tablespoons plus 1 tablespoon butter or olive oil
Pinch of nutmeg
4 cups milk or cream
½ cup sweet onion (preferably Vidalia), diced
¼ cup flour
Salt and pepper
½ cup white cheddar cheese, grated (optional)

1 Boil the potatoes in salted water about 10 minutes or until tender.

2 While potatoes are cooking, sauté the chanterelles at medium temperature in 1 tablespoon olive oil or butter, for about 10 minutes. Add nutmeg and stir. Set aside.

3 When potatoes are done, drain off most of the water. Use a masher to break them into small chunks. Add mushrooms and milk or cream. Return to burner on low and simmer for about 5 minutes.

4 While soup is simmering, melt 2 tablespoons butter or oil in pan. Add the onion and sauté until translucent and soft. Add the flour. Cook for several minutes, until golden brown and thick.

5 By this time, the soup should be simmering nicely. Add the flour and onion mixture to the soup and stir. Continue to stir until the soup thickens, and the flour mix is absorbed. Season with salt and pepper as desired.

6 Ladle into dishes. Sprinkle with cheese, if desired. Serve with a good, crusty bread and salad.

Cliff White

Cantharellus lateritius, p. 102

Enjoy!

"Chicken" 'n Biscuits

by David Yates
Servings: 8
Oven: 350°

1 large onion, chopped
1 tablespoon of olive oil, plus more if necessary
2–3 cups Chicken of the Woods (*Laetiporus sulphureus*, p. 82, or *L. cincinnatus*, p. 81), cleaned and cut into bite-size pieces
3 tablespoons flour
2 cups milk or cream
Salt and pepper
½ teaspoon marjoram
Your favorite biscuit recipe—either from scratch or packaged
1 cup cheddar cheese, grated
Paprika for color

Maxine Stone

1 Saute onion in 1 tablespoon olive oil for about 2 minutes. Add "chicks" and more oil if necessary and cook for about 5 minutes. Remove mushrooms and onion from pan and set aside.

2 Add flour to oil in the pan and stir to mix. Continue stirring over low heat, to make the roux. Be careful not to burn the mixture. Once the roux is cooked to a light brown color, add milk or cream and continue to stir. This will thicken and make a nice white sauce. Add salt, pepper, and marjoram. Add mushroom mixture and cook for a couple of minutes.

3 Make biscuit dough. Drop biscuit dough or arrange cut rounds over all. Sprinkle on cheese. Dust with paprika. Bake for about 45 minutes or until biscuits are brown.

This is true comfort food.

Note: Usually the entire *Laetiporus cincinnatus* can be eaten, as it is tender all the way through. Often only the outer edges of *L. sulphureus* are tender.

"Chicken" Enchiladas

by Tracy Sarver Yates
Servings: 6
Oven: 350°

2 cups Chicken of the Woods, (*Laetiporus sulphureus*, p. 82, or *L. cincinnatus*, p. 81), cleaned and cut into small pieces

3 onions, thinly sliced

2 tablespoons olive oil

12 tortillas

1 15-ounce can (1¾ cup) crushed tomatoes

1 15-ounce can (1¾ cup) tomato sauce

1 can chipotle peppers in adobo sauce (found at international grocery stores)

2 cloves garlic

1 teaspoon paprika, preferably "smoked"

1 teaspoon chili powder

½ teaspoon ground cumin

Salt and pepper

1 cup mozzarella or jack cheese, grated

Sour cream and diced green onions for garnish

1 Sauté mushrooms and onions in olive oil for 5–10 minutes until liquid has evaporated. Divide mushroom mixture into 12 portions and put one portion in each tortilla. Roll tortillas and put in a baking dish, seam side down.

2 In a food processor or blender, puree the crushed tomatoes, tomato sauce, chipotle peppers (start with one pepper, adding more to taste), garlic and spices. Pour over tortillas and sprinkle cheese over all.

3 Bake until golden and bubbly, about ½ hour. Serve on plates with a dollop of sour cream and green onions for garnish.

Note: Usually the entire *Laetiporus cincinnatus* can be eaten, as it is tender all the way through. Often only the outer edges of *L. sulphureus* are tender.

Jon Rapp

Laetiporus cincinnatus, p. 81

"Chicken" with Rosemary and Garlic

by Maxine Stone
Servings: 8

Maxine Stone

1 cup wild rice

3 cups water

2 tablespoons plus
1 tablespoon butter

1 medium onion

2 large garlic cloves

2 cups Chicken of the Woods (*Laetiporus sulphureus*, p. 82, or *L. cincinnatus*, p. 81), cleaned and sliced

¼ cup sherry (or more!)

1 sprig fresh rosemary

Salt and pepper

1 tablespoon capers

1 Boil the wild rice with 1 tablespoon butter and a pinch of salt, covered, on low heat for 55 minutes. Start preparing the remainder of the recipe about 15 minutes before the rice is done.

2 Split the onion down the center from the top, so that it separates into strips instead of rings, and slice. Crush or chop the garlic. Sauté the mushrooms for 5–10 minutes, until almost tender. Add the onions and garlic, and sauté. Add the 2 tablespoons butter, sherry, rosemary, and salt and pepper to taste. Turn the heat down just a bit, and cook until the liquid has evaporated. Remove pan from the heat and toss in the capers.

3 Pile the wild rice onto a serving platter, pile the sautéed mushroom mixture on top, and serve.

This is so good!

Creamed Morels

by Maxine Stone
Servings: 6–8

Steve Adams

2 tablespoons unsalted butter

2 shallots, finely chopped

2 cups fresh or 1 handful dried morels (*Morchella esculenta*, p. 109, or *M. elata*, p. 108), reconstituted (keep the liquid)

1 pint cream (you can use half-and-half, but the cream makes it absolutely superb!)

2–3 tablespoons Marsala

Salt and pepper

1 Melt the butter, add the shallots, and sauté for a few minutes.

2 If using **fresh morels**, cut each one in half lengthwise. Pick out bugs and/or dirt and wash only if necessary. If you have large morels cut them into smaller pieces, but not too small. Add the morels to the sautéed shallots and sauté for a few minutes.

3 If using **dried morels**, reconstitute. Cut them into pieces, but not too small. Squeeze out morel liquid and save. Add the morels to the shallots and sauté for a few minutes. Add the morel liquid, being careful not to pour in the sediment that has fallen to the bottom (could be sand, dirt or bugs).

4 Continue to cook the morels until most of the liquid in the pan has evaporated. Add the cream and cook for a few more minutes until mixture thickens. Add salt and pepper to taste. Add Marsala to taste. Eat and enjoy!

The best way to eat this dish is right from the pan. Grab a piece of good bread then dip and scoop. **It's great participatory food!**

Green Eggs and Ham

by Stan Hudson
Servings: 2

A few indigo milkies (*Lactarius indigo*, p. 52)
1 tablespoon butter
4 eggs
2 slices of ham

1 Clean indigos by wiping away anything stuck to the top. Wash only if necessary. Slice them up and sauté lightly in butter.

2 Fry eggs in the same pan as the indigos. Add ham and heat.

"I often do this for breakfast. The blue stain from the mushrooms should make the eggs green—which, of course, reminds my kids of the Dr. Seuss book *Green Eggs and Ham.*"

Catherine Williamson

Lactarius indigo, p. 52

Grilled Mushrooms

by Ken Gilberg

Young, firm mushrooms, like Hen of the Woods (*Grifola frondosa*, p. 95) or the Lobster (*Hypomyces lactifluorum*, p. 104)

Olive oil

Garlic

Herbs of your choosing

Salt and pepper

1 Slice the mushrooms and marinate in olive oil, garlic and herbs for an hour. Grill. Salt and pepper to taste.

2 Another idea: skewer raw mushrooms and baste them with marinade on the grill. Great for morels.

Note: When you find a fresh "hen," you can slice and eat the entire mushroom, not just the fronds. It's all good.

David Stonner

Hypomyces lactifluorum, p. 104

Hearty "Hen" Soup

by Maxine Stone
Servings: 4–6

Steve Adams

- 2 cups onion, chopped
- 2 tablespoons plus 1 tablespoon butter
- 3 cups Hen of the Woods (*Grifola frondosa*, p. 95), sliced
- 1–2 teaspoons dill weed
- 1½ cups plus ½ cup vegetable stock or water
- 1 tablespoon tamari
- 1–2 tablespoons Hungarian paprika
- 3 tablespoons flour
- 1 cup milk
- 2 teaspoons fresh lemon juice
- Salt and pepper
- Chopped parsley (optional)
- Thick Greek yogurt (optional)

1 Sauté the onion in 1 tablespoon butter over medium heat. Add the mushrooms, dill, ½ cup stock or water, tamari and paprika. Cover and simmer for about 15 minutes.

2 In a large pot, melt 2 tablespoons butter. Whisk in flour and cook a few minutes while continuing to whisk. Add milk. Cook over low heat until thick, stirring frequently, about 10 minutes. Stir in mushroom mixture and 1½ cups stock or water, lemon juice, salt and pepper. Cover and let simmer for about 10 more minutes.

3 Garnish with chopped parsley and/or thick Greek yogurt.

This has a deep, delicious flavor. Serve it with salad and a good bread. **Mmmmm.**

Hericium Salad

by David Yates
Servings: 6

2 cups Hericium (*Hericium coralloides*, p. 120, or *H. erinaceus*, p. 121), cleaned
Juice of 1 lemon
1 green onion, diced
1 stalk celery
½ cup mayonnaise
2 tablespoons rice vinegar
1 teaspoon dill
Salt and pepper

1 Parboil Hericium in water with lemon juice for about 10 minutes. Drain and squeeze out water. Tear or chop Hericium into bite-size pieces. Mix with remaining ingredients in a large bowl. Serve and enjoy.

Believe it or not,
this tastes like crab meat salad.

Steve Adams

Lepiota Beignets

by Françoise Chabot
Adapted from Les Meilleures Recettes de Champignons by Roland Durand
Translated by Patrick Lennon
Servings: 8

Brad Bomanz

Macrolepiota procera, p. 50

8 lepiotas (*Macrolepiota procera*, p. 50) with caps about egg-sized, either closed or open
½ cup flour
2 eggs, separated
1 cup cold milk
1 teaspoon olive oil
2 tablespoons parsley, minced
Salt and pepper
Frying oil
¼ lemon

1 Clean the caps of the lepiotas without washing them, if possible. Cut closed caps into quarters lengthwise; cut opened caps into bite-size pieces.

2 To make the batter, first place the flour in a bowl. Make a depression in the flour and add the egg yolks. Mix with a whisk while adding the milk and olive oil little by little. Beat the egg whites until they are firm, and incorporate them and the minced parsley rapidly into the flour mixture. Add salt and pepper.

3 Heat the frying oil. Dip each lepiota piece separately into the batter, then carefully drop into the hot oil. Turn the pieces gently so that they brown evenly.

4 When they are golden all over, remove the beignets to a serving platter lined with paper towels. Squeeze a couple drops of lemon juice on each beignet. Enjoy!

In French, beignet means doughnut. I hope you're lucky enough to collect eight good-looking *Macrolepiota procera* caps so that you can try these delicious "doughnuts."

"Lobster" and Green Bean Salad with Goat Cheese

by David Yates
Servings: 6

1 pound haricot vert or other slender green beans, ends trimmed
4 tablespoons plus 3 tablespoons extra-virgin olive oil
2 tablespoons balsamic vinegar
1 tablespoon fresh thyme, chopped
Salt and pepper
1 pound fresh lobster mushrooms (*Hypomyces lactifluorum*, p. 104), sliced
1 large shallot, chopped
3 ounces soft, mild goat cheese (such as Montrachet), crumbled

1 Steam beans over water until crisp-tender, about 4 minutes. Drain. Transfer to bowl of ice water. Cool and drain well. Pat dry with paper towel. Set aside.

2 Whisk 4 tablespoons olive oil, vinegar and thyme in small bowl. Add salt and pepper to taste. Set dressing aside.

3 Heat remaining 3 tablespoons oil in large skillet over medium heat. Add mushrooms and shallot. Sauté until mushrooms are brown and tender, about 8 minutes. Remove from heat.

4 Combine beans and mushrooms in a beautiful bowl. Pour dressing over all. Sprinkle with goat cheese and serve.

Maxine Stone

Morgan's Chanterelles

by Morgan Johnson (Maxine's granddaughter)

1–2 tablespoons butter
1 clove garlic, sliced
1 cup fresh chanterelles (*Cantharellus cibarius*, p. 100, or *C. lateritius*, p. 102), torn into pieces
Splash balsamic vinegar
Salt and pepper
Bread, pasta or rice

1 Melt butter with garlic and sauté until garlic is soft. Add chanterelles. Let them sauté for 4–5 minutes. Add a splash of balsamic vinegar, and salt and pepper. Continue to cook until done. Serve over rice (good), pasta (better), or bread (best). Enjoy.

Steve Adams

"My dad ate the whole thing."

"Oysters" Rockefeller

by David Yates
Servings: 8
Oven: 425°

Steve Adams

2–3 cups oyster mushrooms (*Pleurotus ostreatus*, p. 90, or *P. pulmonarius*, p. 90), cut to resemble oyster shells
¾ cup beer
1 clove garlic
Salt
3–4 whole black peppercorns
2 tablespoons butter
1 onion, chopped
1 clove garlic, minced
1 10-ounce package frozen chopped spinach, thawed and drained
¼ cup Monterey Jack cheese, shredded
¼ cup fontina cheese, shredded
¼ cup mozzarella cheese, shredded
¼ cup milk
Salt and pepper
½ cup seasoned bread crumbs

This is sinfully good.

1 Put mushrooms in a large pot. Pour in beer and enough water to cover. Add garlic, salt and peppercorns. Bring to a boil and simmer for about 5 minutes. Remove from heat, drain, and cool. Arrange the oysters on a baking sheet.

2 Melt butter in a pan over medium heat. Cook onion and garlic in butter until soft. Reduce heat to low, and stir in spinach, Monterey Jack, fontina, and mozzarella. Cook until cheese melts, stirring frequently. Stir in the milk, and season with salt and pepper. Spoon sauce over each oyster, as if you were filling a real oyster shell. Sprinkle with bread crumbs.

3 Bake 8–10 minutes, until golden and bubbly.

Pickled "Hens"—Italian Style

by Stevie Booker
Servings: 6–8

8 cups Hen of the Woods (*Grifola frondosa*, p. 95), cleaned and separated
¼ cup fresh lemon juice
1 onion
2 green peppers
1 red pepper
1 yellow pepper
6 cloves garlic, either chopped or whole
6 anchovy fillets, mashed or crumbled
6 cups water
2 cups vinegar
1½ cups sugar

1 Place hen pieces in pot and cover with water. Add lemon juice. Bring to a boil and simmer for about 10 minutes. Rinse in cool water and set aside.

2 Cut onion and peppers into bite-size pieces. Add garlic and anchovies. Put everything, including mushrooms, into a large pot and add water, vinegar and sugar. Bring to a boil and simmer for about 10 minutes. Remove from heat and cool. Put into clean jars and refrigerate for a week or so before eating.

Steve Adams

Enjoy this as an appetizer or a flavorful side dish.

Pickled Stinkhorn Eggs

by Shannon Stevens

Stinkhorn eggs (*Phallus ravenelii*, p. 129, or *Mutinus elegans*, p. 128), as many as you can find
Juice from bread-and-butter, dill or other pickles

1 Before beginning this project, cut one of your "eggs" open to be sure it hasn't started turning into a Stinkhorn yet. If it's too far along, don't use them.

2 Put juice and "eggs" in a clean jar. Let sit in the refrigerator for a couple of months. Take out, cut into pieces and share with friends.

Brad Bomanz

Phallus ravenelii , p. 129

There is definitely a sense of pride when you eat stinkhorn eggs and join a very select group of mycophagists who have tried **this delicacy.**

Puffball, Peppers and Parmesan

by Maxine Stone
Servings: 4–6
Oven: 350°

1 medium Giant Puffball
(*Calvatia gigantea*, p. 112)
Olive oil for sautéing and baking
¼ cup balsamic vinegar
3 large shallots or small onions
¼ cup vegetable or chicken broth
2 tablespoons dry sherry
1 jar roasted red peppers
½ cup grated mozzarella cheese
½ cup good parmesan cheese
Pinch basil
Pinch oregano

Tim Gleason
Calvatia gigantea, p. 112

1 Cut puffball down the center and make sure there is no sign of a cap or stem. Slice the puffball into ¼" slabs. Heat olive oil in a large non-stick pan. Place the puffball slices in the pan and dribble balsamic vinegar on each slice as it cooks. Sauté the puffball slices for a few minutes on each side until slightly brown. The vinegar should evaporate and caramelize. Set them aside. (Optional—you can bread the puffball slabs before you cook them.)

2 Slice the shallots vertically into thin slices. Pour a bit more olive oil into the pan, heat, and add shallots. Cook shallots for a few minutes, until they start to turn golden and translucent. Add broth and sherry. Cook until liquid is almost absorbed. Carefully remove the shallots as they cook and soften.

3 Spread a film of olive oil onto a baking tray. Place a thin layer of roasted red peppers, then a layer of puffballs, then slices of cooked shallot. Sprinkle with mozzarella, parmesan, basil and oregano. Continue to layer until all ingredients have been used. Bake until the cheese melts and all is bubbly, about 30 minutes.

The ingredients meld beautifully and it tastes wonderful!

Salmon with Black Trumpet Sauce

by Maxine Stone
Servings: 4

4 salmon fillets
 (¼ lb. each, skinned if possible)

2 tablespoons fresh orange juice

Salt

2 cups fresh black trumpets
 (*Craterellus cornucopioides*, p. 103)
 or ⅔ cups dried and rehydrated

2 tablespoons butter plus
 1 tablespoon butter for grilling

1 clove garlic, minced

½ cup leeks, sliced, plus leek
 greens for garnish

½ cup vegetable stock

½ cup dry white wine

¼ cup cream or half-and-half

Salt and pepper

Orange zest

Maxine Stone

1 Put the salmon on a plate and cover with the orange juice. Sprinkle with salt and set aside.

2 Cut the trumpets into bite-size pieces. Melt 2 tablespoons butter and add the garlic. Sauté for a few seconds, then add the mushrooms. When the mushrooms are cooked, stir in the sliced leeks until wilted and dark. Add the stock and wine and reduce by half.

3 While the sauce is reducing, melt 1 tablespoon butter in a grilling pan. Grill the salmon for a couple of minutes on each side, depending on your desired doneness.

4 When the sauce is reduced, add the cream or half-and-half and season with salt and freshly ground black pepper to taste.

5 Spoon the mushroom sauce onto plates and place the salmon on top. Garnish with finely cut leek greens and/or orange zest.

The color is gorgeous, the taste is superb!

Self-crusting Chanterelle Quiche

by Maxine Stone
Servings: 4–6
Oven: 400°

1 medium onion, chopped
2 tablespoons unsalted butter, divided
2 cups chanterelles (*Cantharellus cibarius*, p. 100, or *C. lateritius*, p. 102), cleaned and torn into bite-size pieces
1 cup red pepper or other vegetables, cut into bite-size pieces (optional)
1 cup shredded good-quality parmesan or asiago cheese
1½ cups milk
¾ cup biscuit mix (preferably with no artificial ingredients—can be purchased at health food stores)
3 eggs
Salt and pepper to taste
Fresh herbs to taste—basil or dill or rosemary or whatever you have

1 Grease or spray a 10-inch quiche pan or pie pan.

2 Sauté onions in one tablespoon butter until they begin to brown. Add the other tablespoon of butter, the chanterelles, and the vegetables if desired. Sauté until mushrooms and vegetables soften and liquid has evaporated.

3 Cover bottom of prepared pan with mushrooms and vegetables. Beat all the other ingredients until smooth. Pour over mushrooms and vegetables. Bake 30–35 minutes. Cool 5–10 minutes and serve.

This easy quiche is **delicious** hot, or at room temperature.

Cliff White

Cantharellus lateritius, p. 102

Shrimp Parmesan with Cinnabar Chanterelle Garni

by Donna Harvey
Servings: 4

2 tablespoons butter
3 cloves roasted garlic, mashed
1 teaspoon fresh basil
1 pound medium shrimp, peeled and de-veined
1 pound fresh asparagus, cut in 2-inch pieces and lightly steamed
4 cups cooked pasta
½–1 cup parmigiano reggiano, grated
½ cup cream or half-and-half
Salt and pepper
1 cup Cinnabar Chanterelles (*Cantharellus cinnabarinus*, p. 101)
¼ cup olive oil

1 Melt butter in a large pan. Add garlic and basil and sauté 2–3 minutes. Add shrimp and asparagus and sauté gently until shrimp is cooked. Add pasta, reggiano and cream or half-and-half. Simmer mixture for 3–4 minutes, being careful not to boil, until sauce starts to thicken. Add salt and pepper to taste.

2 In another pan, dry sauté the mushrooms over low heat until most of the moisture is out, about 10 minutes. Remove mushrooms and add olive oil to the pan. Heat oil and add mushrooms back to the pan in small batches, cooking until crisp.

3 Serve the shrimp parmesan in a beautiful bowl. Garnish with mushrooms and sprinkle a little more reggiano on top.

Jon Rapp

Cantharellus cinnabarinus, p. 101

A simple and fantastic meal!

Sparassis or Candy Cap Sauce

by David Yates and Maxine Stone
Servings: 6–8

Steve Adams

- 2 cups *Sparassis spatulata*, p. 97 (if you're lucky enough to find one) or 2 ounces dried candy caps*
- ¼ cup butter
- 2 egg yolks
- ½ cup brown sugar
- ½ cup granulated sugar
- 1 teaspoon vanilla
- Pinch nutmeg
- Pinch allspice
- ½ cup walnuts, chopped and toasted (optional)

1 If using **Sparassis**, clean and cut into small pieces. Parboil in water for 5–10 minutes. Drain, but keep ½ cup cooking liquid. Pat dry.

2 If using **candy caps**, soak in warm water for at least ½ hour. Drain, but keep ½ cup soaking liquid, making sure sandy residue isn't included. Cut into small pieces.

3 Melt butter in pan. Add mushrooms, and sauté for a few minutes. Add the cooking or soaking liquid, and the egg yolks, brown sugar, granulated sugar, vanilla, nutmeg and allspice. Mix and cook over medium heat, stirring constantly until mixture thickens and begins to boil. (If necessary, add one tablespoon real maple syrup.) Boil gently for 1 minute. Turn off heat and add toasted walnuts. Serve either warm or cool over a good quality vanilla ice cream.

It's pretty awesome that a wild mushroom can be a **delicious dessert.**

* *The Candy Cap (*Lactarius rubidus*) doesn't grow in Missouri, and in the U.S. is found only on the West Coast. When dried, it has a wonderful maple-sugary taste and fragrance. If you aren't heading west any time soon, dried candy caps can be purchased from mushroom sellers at farmer's markets and online.*

Bernadette Dryden

Glossary

Agaric—A gilled mushroom (in the Order Agaricales)

Bolete—A pored mushroom (in the Order Boletales) with a circular cap and central stem, and a pore layer on the cap underside that can be easily separated from the cap

Bruising—The tendency of certain mushrooms to discolor when pressed firmly

Cap—The part of a mushroom that sits at the top of the stalk and has spore-producing structures such as gills or pores

Cluster—A group of the same species of fungi growing close together

Concave—With the center lower than the outside edge; rounded downward; refers to the shape of a mushroom cap

Coniferous—Cone-bearing; usually refers to evergreen trees

Conk—a woody, perennial fungus on a living or dead tree

Convex—With the center higher than the outside edge; rounded upward; refers to the shape of a mushroom cap

Cup fungi—Fungi that form spores on the surface of cup- or goblet-like fruiting bodies

Deciduous—Shedding its leaves in the fall

Depressed—With a sunken center; refers to the shape of a mushroom cap

Descending—Running from the underside of the cap down the stalk; refers to mushroom gills

Egg—Common name for the small, round, spore-bearing structures in bird's-nest fungi; also may refer to an immature stinkhorn, or an immature amanita before the universal veil is broken.

Ellipsoid—Like an ellipse; football-shaped; refers to mushroom spores

Fairy ring—A ring of mushrooms that forms at the outer edge of a growing mycelium; usually found in lawns or meadows

Flesh—The interior tissue of the fruiting body of a fungus

Fleshy—Referring to a fruiting body in which the interior tissue is thick and the consistency of flesh

Fruiting body—The part of a fungus that produces spores; a mushroom

Fungus—An organism belonging to the Kingdom Fungi, and consisting of a mycelium on which fruiting bodies are produced

Gills—The bladelike structures that hang from the underside of a mushroom cap, and are the sites where spores are produced

Host—The living plant or animal on which a parasitic or saprophytic fungus feeds

Hyphae—The threadlike filaments that make up the mycelium of a fungus

Incurved—With the edge turned in toward the center; refers to a mushroom cap or cup

Latex—A thick, milky juice exuded by *Lactarius* mushrooms when cut or broken

Margin—The free edge of a mushroom cap or gill

Marginate—Gills with margins that are a different color than the flat surfaces

Milky—A mushroom in the genus *Lactarius*, which oozes a white or colored latex

Mycologist—A person who studies fungi as a vocation; a mushroom expert

Mycophile—A person who enjoys collecting, studying and/or eating fungi

Mushroom—The fruiting body of a fungus

Mycelium—A network of hyphae, growing in soil, on wood, or on some other substrate, that makes up the vegetative portion of a fungus.

Mycology—The study of fungi

Mycorrhizal—growing in the symbiotic association formed when fungal hyphae surround the rootlets of a tree, allowing both to obtain nutrients more effectively

Parasitic—Feeding on another living organism in a way that does harm to that organism

Partial veil—A membrane that extends from the edge of the cap to the stalk, protecting the developing gills; found in immature mushrooms of some species

Polypore—A pored mushroom (in the Order Polyporales) with a fleshy, leathery, or woody cap, a stalk that is off-center or absent, and a pore layer on the cap underside that cannot be separated from the cap

Pore—The mouth of one of the tiny, spore-producing tubes that cover the undersides of polypores and boletes

Rhizomorph—A cordlike strand of mycelium

Ring—The remnants of a partial veil on the stalk of a mushroom

Saprophytic—Feeding on dead organic matter

Scale—A small tear or separation on the surface of a mushroom cap or stalk; can be flattened or erect

Shelf—A stalkless fungus, usually a polypore, which grows out of a wood surface

Spore—The microscopic "seed" of a fungus

Spore print—The pattern made by spores when a mature mushroom cap is placed, gill side down, on paper (see page 21)

Stalk—The stem of a mushroom; may be attached in the center of the cap (central) or closer to the margin (off-center)

Substrate—The material on which a mycelium or fruiting body is growing

Symbiosis—Two organisms growing together in a way that benefits both

Toadstool—The folk name for a poisonous mushroom

Tube—One of the tiny, spore-producing structures that cover the undersides of polypores and boletes

Universal veil—The membrane or tissue that, in some mushroom species, completely covers the immature mushroom

Veil—A membrane that covers part or all of a developing mushroom

Volva—The remains of the universal veil, left as a cup at the base of the stalk

Zoned—With concentric rings of different colors and/or textures

Mushrooms by Edibility Category

Choice through Edible

★★★★ CHOICE

Agaricus campestris	Meadow Mushroom	⚠ (with caution)
Calvatia gigantea	Giant Puffball	⚠ (with caution)
Cantharellus cibarius	Chanterelle	⚠ (with caution)
Cantharellus lateritius	Smooth Chanterelle	⚠ (with caution)
Coprinus comatus	Shaggy Mane	
Craterellus cornucopioides	Black Trumpet	
Grifola frondosa	Hen of the Woods	℞ (medicinal)
Hericium erinaceus	Bearded Tooth	
Hericium coralloides	Comb Tooth	
Hydnum repandum	Hedgehog	
Hypomyces lactifluorum	Lobster Mushroom	
Lactarius hygrophoroides	Hygrophorus Milky	
Lactarius volemus	Voluminous-latex Milky	
Laetiporus cincinnatus	Chicken of the Woods	
Laetiporus sulphureus	Chicken of the Woods	
Lepista nuda	Blewit	
Macrolepiota procera	Parasol	⚠ (with caution)
Morchella elata	Black Morel	
Morchella esculenta	Yellow Morel	
Pleurotus ostreatus, P. pulmonarius	Oyster Mushroom	

★★★ Excellent

Bondarzewia berkeleyi	Berkeley's Polypore	
Lactarius indigo	Indigo Milky	
Lycoperdon perlatum	Gem-studded Puffball	⚠ (with caution)
Lycoperdon pyriforme	Pear-shaped Puffball	⚠ (with caution)
Morchella semilibera	Half-free Morel	
Russula virescens	Green Cracking Russula	
Sparassis spatulata	Eastern Cauliflower Mushroom	

★★ Good

Armillaria mellea	Honey Mushroom	
Armillaria tabescens	Ringless Honey Mushroom	
Cantharellus cinnabarinus	Cinnabar Chanterelle	
Coprinopsis atramentaria	Alcohol Inky	⚠ (with caution)
Fistulina hepatica	Beefsteak Polypore	
Ischnoderma resinosum	Resinous Polypore	
Laccaria ochropurpurea	Purple-gilled Laccaria	
Lepiota americana	Reddening Lepiota	⚠ (with caution)
Meripilus sumstinei	Black-staining Polypore	
Mutinus elegans	Elegant Stinkhorn	⚠ (with caution)
Phallus ravenelii	Ravenel's Stinkhorn	⚠ (with caution)
Polyporus squamosus	Dryad's Saddle	
Xerula radicata	Rooted Collybia	

★ Edible

Artomyces pyxidatus	Crown-tipped Coral	⚠ (with caution)
Auricularia auricula-judae	Wood Ear	℞ (medicinal)
Boletinellus merulioides	Ash-tree Bolete	
Boletus pallidus	Pallid Bolete	
Coprinellus micaceus	Mica Cap	
Ganoderma lucidum	Ling Chih	℞ (medicinal)
Hygrocybe coccinea	Scarlet Waxy Cap	
Laccaria laccata	Common Laccaria	
Lactarius piperatus	Peppery Milky	
Marasmius oreades	Fairy Ring Mushroom	⚠ (with caution)
Polyporus alveolaris	Hexagonal-pored Polypore	
Pluteus atricapillus	Fawn Mushroom	⚠ (with caution)
Strobilomyces floccopus, S. confusus	Old Man of the Woods, Confusing Old Man of the Woods	
Trametes versicolor	Turkey Tail	℞ (medicinal)
Tremella mesenterica	Witches' Butter	

Continued on next page

Continued from previous page

Not Recommended through Deadly

Not Recommended

Amanita citrina	Citron Amanita
Amanita rubescens	Blusher
Amanita vaginata	Grisette
Boletus bicolor	Two-colored Bolete
Boletus frostii	Frost's Bolete
Cortinarius alboviolaceus	Silvery-violet Cort
Flammulina velutipes	Velvet Foot

Not Edible

Amanita flavoconia	Yellow Patches
Amanita onusta	Onusta Amanita
Amanita thiersii	Thiers Amanita
Cyathus striatus	Splash Cup
Daedaleopsis confragosa	Thin-maze Flat Polypore
Exidia alba	Pale Jelly Roll
Galiella rufa	Hairy Rubber Cup
Ganoderma applanatum	Artist Conk
Geastrum spp.	Earthstar
Lenzites betulina	Multi-color Gill Polypore
Leotia lubrica	Jelly Baby
Lycogala epidendrum	Wolf's-milk Slime
Marasmius siccus	Orange Pinwheel Marasmius
Mycena haematopus	Bleeding Mycena
Mycena leaiana	Orange Mycena
Phlebia incarnata	Coral-pink Merulius
Polyporus badius	Black-footed Polypore
Polyporus radicatus	Rooting Polypore
Pycnoporus cinnabarinus	Cinnabar Polypore

✕ Not Edible, *continued*

Sarcoscypha dudleyi	Scarlet Cup
Sarcoscypha occidentalis	Stalked Scarlet Cup
Schizophyllum commune	Common Split Gill
Stereum ostrea	False Turkey Tail
Tremellodendron pallidum	Jellied False Coral
Trichaptum biforme	Violet Toothed Polypore
Tylopilus felleus	Bitter Bolete
Tylopilus plumbeoviolaceus	Violet-gray Bolete
Urnula craterium	Devil's Urn
Xylaria polymorpha	Dead Man's Fingers

Poisonous

Chlorophyllum molybdites	Green-spored Lepiota
Gymnopilus junonius	Big Laughing Gym
Omphalotus illudens	Jack O'Lantern
Russula emetica	Emetic Russula
Scleroderma citrinum	Pigskin Puffball

DEADLY

Amanita bisporigera	Destroying Angel
Galerina autumnalis	Deadly Galerina
Gyromitra brunnea	Gabled False Morel
Gyromitra caroliniana	Big Red False Morel

Bibliography

Field Guides to North American Mushrooms

A Field Guide to Mushrooms: North America (Peterson Field Guide Series)
By Kent H. McKnight and Vera B. McKnight

Mushrooms and Other Fungi of North America
By Roger Phillips

Mushrooms of Northeast North America: Midwest to New England
By George Barron

National Audubon Society Field Guide to North American Mushrooms
By Gary H. Lincoff

North American Mushrooms: A Field Guide to Edible and Inedible Fungi
By Orson K. Miller Jr. and Hope H. Miller

Other Useful Mushroom Books

100 Edible Mushrooms
By Michael Kuo

All That the Rain Promises and More
By David Arora

Edible Wild Mushrooms of Illinois and Surrounding States: A Field-to-Kitchen Guide
By Joe McFarland and Gregory M. Mueller

Morels
By Michael Kuo

Mushrooms Demystified
By David Arora

The Pocket Guide to Mushrooms
By Jean Marie Polese

Websites

MushroomExpert.com

TomVolkFungi.net

Cliff White

Amanita flavoconia, p. 41

Index

D

E

F

Boletus frostii, p. 66

Field Notes

Field Notes

Field Notes